Laurence F. Renehan, Daniel McCarthy

Collections on Irish Church History

Volume II: Irish Archbishops

Laurence F. Renehan, Daniel McCarthy

Collections on Irish Church History
Volume II: Irish Archbishops

ISBN/EAN: 9783337201760

Printed in Europe, USA, Canada, Australia, Japan

Cover: Foto ©ninafisch / pixelio.de

More available books at **www.hansebooks.com**

COLLECTIONS

ON

IRISH CHURCH HISTORY.

FROM THE MSS. OF THE LATE
VERY REV. LAURENCE F. RENEHAN, D.D.,
President of Maynooth College.

EDITED BY
THE REV. DANIEL M'CARTHY, D.D.,
Professor of S. Scriptures, Maynooth.

VOL. II.
IRISH BISHOPS.

Remember your Prelates who have spoken the word of God to you; whose faith follow, considering the end of their conversation—Heb. xiii. 7.

DUBLIN:
JAMES DUFFY AND SONS, 15 WELLINGTON QUAY,
AND 22 PATERNOSTER ROW, LONDON.
LONDON: BURNS, OATES, AND CO., 17 PORTMAN STREET.
1873.

TO

THE MOST REVEREND

THE BISHOPS OF IRELAND,

THIS VOLUME

IS

HUMBLY INSCRIBED.

PREFACE.

In the Preface to the first volume of these COLLECTIONS I explained so fully the nature of my design, that I deem it superfluous to say much on the same subject again here.

1. This volume, like the first on the Archbishops, is taken chiefly from the O'RENEHAN MSS, bequeathed by the late President of Maynooth to the College Trustees. In preparing it for press, I found it necessary to make so many changes that I abandoned the idea of giving Dr. Renehan's own words, and marking the additional matter by brackets. To meet, however, the wishes of such readers as may wish to consult the original papers, I shall insert at the end of the volume the index of the O'Renehan MSS, which I made for my own use and facility of reference. By consulting it, what has been added by the Editor may be easily known.

2. I propose to give in this volume brief notices of the Irish Bishops *since* the Reformation. Of the canonically elected bishops in Ireland *during the Reformation period*, that is, from 1536 to 1600, I wrote a short account in an essay appended to Dr. Kelly's DISSERTATIONS, published by Mr. Duffy in 1864. And though great light has been since thrown on their history by the learned Bishop of Ossory, in the *Irish Record*, and by Dr. Maziere Brady, in his able and exhaustive pamphlet on the "*Irish Reformation*", I do not think it expedient to go over the

same ground again. I shall therefore begin with the Bishops appointed after 1600, and trace the succession in each diocese down to our own time. The task is a most difficult one; that I must have failed often is quite certain, "but to fail in great designs is a noble fault".

3. At the suggestion of many esteemed friends, I have resolved to print each Part separately, in the hope that some at least, whose limited means preclude the purchase of a costly book, would gladly procure the Part that treats of their own diocese, and so remember and imitate the faith and conversation of the prelates who spake unto them the word of God.

Maynooth College, Dec. 1, 1873.

WORKS EDITED BY THE REV. DR. M'CARTHY.

1. COLLECTIONS ON IRISH CHURCH HISTORY. By the Very Rev. L. F. RENEHAN, D.D., President of Maynooth. Vol. I., IRISH ARCHBISHOPS. Dublin: Duffy. 7s. 6d.

2. HISTORY OF MUSIC. By the same. Dublin: Warren, Ormond Quay. 2s. 6d.

3. DISSERTATIONS ON IRISH HISTORY. By the Rev. M. KELLY, D.D., Professor of Ecclesiastical History, Maynooth College. Dublin: Duffy. 7s. d6.

4. LOGICÆ SEU PHILOSOPHIÆ RATIONALIS COMPENDIUM. Cura Rev. GULIELMI JENNINGS, Philosophiæ Prof. in R. C. Collegio S. Patricii apud Maynooth. Dublin: Gill. 3s. 6d.

5. THE EPISTLES AND GOSPELS OF THE SUNDAYS THROUGHOUT THE YEAR, with Notes, Critical and Explanatory. By the Rev DANIEL M'CARTHY, D.D., Professor of Sacred Scripture and Hebrew, Maynooth College. Dublin: Duffy. Vol. I. EPISTLES (Two Parts), 12s. Vol. II. GOSPELS (Two Parts), 10s.

COLLECTIONS

ON

IRISH CHURCH HISTORY,

BISHOPS OF FERNS.

JOHN ROCHE, *suc.* 1627; *ob.* 1636.

THE see of Ferns had been vacant from the death of Peter Power in 1587 (1588 Bruodin) until the accession of John Roche, a secular priest, and, I think, a native of the diocese. James Walshe, reputed Bishop in 1613 according to Fitzgerald's narrative (MS. T.C.D.), and the Royal Visitation in the Irish Academy Library, was merely vicar and missionary-apostolic. From Dr. Roche's close friendship and frequent correspondence (some of which is preserved among the MSS. of St. Isidore's) with the celebrated Luke Wadding, I am inclined to believe that he must have been acquainted with Wadding in Lisbon or Rome, and perhaps his fellow-student or pupil. The date usually assigned for his appointment to the see of Ferns is 1626 or 1627, but no decisive evidence has been quoted yet to fix either year. The earliest authentic document that I can refer to with his name as Bishop is the following letter to Wadding, dated Paris, Oct. 20, 1628:

Rt. Rev. Father,—As your sickness, which was written to me by Sign. Eug., and Sign. Gio. Bapti. from my Lord Cardinal's house, has made me pensive for your health, so the news of your perfect recovery, which by the self Don Giov. Bapti. is signified to me, doth make me very glad. These are, therefore, to testify unto you my joy of your foresaid recovery, with my prayers for your continuance and increase in it. . . . What shall I write to you of Rochel? The English be here still, and have done nothing. . . . The letters from London do bring word that in the sessions of Aug. two priests were put to death, one in Chester and the other in Lincoln, and two laymen, for persuading others to become Catholics. We did not think that the Proclamation, which issued on the complaints of the Puritans in Parliament against Catholics would be put in execution, but we see that the reasons which induced the king to make the Proclamation, viz., the greedy perverseness of the Puritans, made him also give way to the execution. . . . Commend me, I pray you, to the good company of St. Isidore's. I hope we shall soon get passage. I am myself, and will ever be, your assured servant—J. Roche, *Fernensis*.

The next paper with his name is a letter to Propaganda of Feb. 9, 1629, praying their Eminences to appoint three Bishops in England, as one was not able to attend to the urgent wants of the people. This petition is signed by Thomas Casbel, William Cork, Richard Limerick, Maurice Emly, Francis Waterford and Lismore, David Ossory, and *John Ferns*.

Dr. Roche took an active part in the bitter and protracted struggle between Dr. Cahill, P.P. of SS.

Michael and John's, Dublin, and his archbishop, Dr. Fleming, if we can rely upon the unsupported testimony of Paul Harris. The Rev. Patrick Cahill was a native of Meath, affiliated to Dublin, and P.P. of SS. Michael and John's. When deprived of his parish by Dr. Fleming, a *Franciscan* Bishop, he brought a charge against the Regular clergy of Dublin, of false doctrine, which he embodied in eleven propositions, and submitted to the college of Sorbonne. That the propositions were justly censured by that learned faculty, though perhaps it was not their province to decide, cannot be questioned, but that they had been ever maintained by any person in Ireland, lay or clerical, is more than doubtful. Yet Cahill, aided by three discontented priests, repeated the calumny in Rome, whither he went to prosecute his appeal against Archbishop Fleming. He got letters of introduction from Dr. Roche to his friends, and, according to Paul Harris (Arklomastix, p. 33), most excellent testimonials. Harris also states that he brought with him letters from the Bishops of Armagh, Ossory, Ferns, Cork, Meath, and Kilmore. The Roman authorities ordered an inquiry to be made by four Irish Bishops, two of them being regulars. After several months the Cardinals received the report of the Irish Commission, and letters signed by the four Archbishops of Ireland and *almost* all their suffragans, stating that no such doctrine had been ever publicly or privately taught in their dioceses, and that no regular ever maintained the condemned propositions. It was decreed, therefore, in Jan., 1632, to forbid the circulation of these propositions, or to impute them to the Friars. By the same decree was forbidden a book styled *The*

Dialogue of Nicephorus, written in French, translated into English, and studiously circulated by Cahill. This work contained a series of insidious attacks on the various religious orders in Ireland. A full account of the dispute may be seen in Wadding's Annals, tom. viii, an. 1357, n. 15, from whose words we cannot conclusively prove that Dr. Roche did not favour Cahill, but they show that Harris' statements are false and libellous in most important particulars, and therefore not to be relied upon in other respects. I find that Dr. Roche assisted at the Synod of Kilkenny in the month of Aug. 1628 (Harris, p. 57), and was joined therein by the Archbishops of Dublin and Cashel, and by the Bishops of Ossory, Cork, and Waterford. At this meeting Paul Harris denounced a book written by the Rev. Thos. Strong, O.S.F., and appealed to the bishops to censure it; but they referred the matter to the Archbishop of Dublin, in whose diocese the book had been published, where the author lived, and where the so-called errors had been preached. Though Harris seems to have been bitterly hostile to all religious societies, and to his archbishop for his connection with them, and to have made this controversy a kind of party warfare between seculars and regulars, it was not from such feeling that Dr. Roche gave him or Cahill the least countenance or support. Among the Irish bishops there was not one, except Dr. Cullinane of Raphoe, who showed more kindness to regulars of every institute. Malachy Hartry gratefully acknowledges the obligations of his own Cistercians to the Bishop of Ferns, who was their friend and patron when they needed much his protection. He always speaks of him with profound respect, and records his death thus: Revmus. D. Joannes Roche, Epus. Fernensis, doctrina, humanitateque insignis obiit 10 Aprilis, 1636. *M.S. Triumphalia S. Crucis.* Another strong testimony to the bishop's zeal is given incidentally by Justice Cressy, who sent a report of the state of Wexford to the Deputy Strafford after the assizes, Aug. 1633, complaining, " that the most ancient English plantators are now Romish and Popish. . . . all recusants, not one Protestant amongst them", and promising " to do all he could to prevent the policy of the priests. I shall this day press them to find their bishop here placed amongst them by the Pope's authority".

It is plain that the bishop was regarded as the chief author of the great change which brought over the oldest Protestant planters to the true faith, and if he were arrested, the pious judge expected to find fewer Popish perverts.

After the death of Dr. Roche in 1636, the Archbishop of Dublin, Dr. Fleming, appointed the Rev. William Devereux vicar of the diocese, and the provincial council held at Tyrchoghir, in the county Kildare, on the 29th July, 1640, published a declaration to the effect that Dr. Devereux thus appointed was truly Ordinary of the diocese, and possessed all the faculties for administering the sacraments usually granted to the missionaries (priests) of Ireland. Dr. Devereux governed the see of Ferns by virtue of this delegation until 1643, when Dr. French was made bishop. *Constitut. Dublinienses,* pp. 78-79.

NICHOLAS FRENCH, *suc.* 1645; *ob.* 1678.

The founder of the French family in this county was Patrick French, who obtained large tracts of land in Wexford soon after the Anglo-Norman invasion, and built the castle of Ballytory, near the town of Broadway in the barony of Forth. From him are descended the Frenches of Castle French, county Galway, who have been the recognized head of the sept ever since they settled in the west, about 1421 (Lodge). " In an inquisition taken in 1616, Robert French of Ballytory is described as seized of the lands of Ballytory. . . . Another inquisition taken in 1637, describes Patrick French, merchant, of Wexford, as seized of all the messuages and seven acres of land in the insula called our Lady's Island. . . . There can be no doubt that the Frenches joined the Confederates at a very early period, for the 'Book of survey and distributions' informs us that Nicholas French (probably the bishop's father) was attainted of rebellion in 1641, and dispossessed of 174 acres, 1 rood, and 26 perches in the parish of Tacumshane, all of which were granted to Neale and Barrington by that most iniquitous fraud called the Act of Settlement in the reign of Charles II." Letter of Rev. C. P. Meehan, published Feb., 1846. Ballytory castle was thus the chief family seat, and hence it has been inferred that N. French was born there. On the other hand Harris (Ware's *Writers*, p. 166) states distinctly that he was born in the town of Wexford. P. Walsh says (*Remon.*, p. 613), speaking of him as P.P. of Wexford " of which place, *I think*, he was a native". In the letter which we publish *infra*, the bishop himself calls Wexford *urbs gentilitia*, his family, or tribe city. But the point is not of great impórtance : he was born in Wexford or near it. From the same letter it appears that he was born in 1603. He studied in the Pastoral College of the Irish at Louvain, where he became successively professor and president, and where he at a later period founded a burse of 180 florins for the support of candidates for the ministry, to be chosen in the first place from his relatives in Wexford, and in their default from all Ireland. See Report of Dr. Higgins' Correspondence with the Belgian Government on Irish Ecclesiastical Property, p. 12. On his return to his native diocese he was appointed P.P. of Wexford, and while such, was elected a burgess of the general assembly at Kilkenny. Not long after he was raised to the episcopal bench in 1645. Harris says he was made titular Bishop of Ferns in 1643, but this early date has been fully disproved by the Rev. Mr. Meehan in the letter already cited. For, first, P. Walsh, who knew Dr. French intimately, asserts that he was promoted to the see of Ferns by Innocent X., who was not appointed Pope until 1644. Secondly, there is still extant the decision given, Oct., 1645, by six theologians, who were consulted on the obligation of 'Titius' (the usual fictitious name in cases of conscience) to accept the bishopric of *Ferns*. Therefore the see was then vacant. Thirdly, the Nuncio Rinuccini wrote from Kilkenny, Nov. 28, 1645, that Fr. Scarampi was then assisting at the consecration of a bishop at Wexford. This last document fixes the date of Dr. French's consecration exactly, if we can but show that he was the bishop referred to by the Nuncio. Now, this is

most likely, for the high terms of praise bestowed by
Rinuccini on the new bishop would hardly be applied
to any one but a special favourite such as Dr. French
always was. I have before me the answer of the
theologians to the case proposed to them, and every
line of it, extending over four folio pages, points to
Dr. French as "Titius", of whose obligation to accept
the mitre the proposed question treats.

He was chancellor of the synod of Waterford in
1646, and a leading promoter of its decrees. He
was also a member of the supreme council at Kilkenny, and sent by the general assembly of the Confederation as ambassador to Rome in 1647 with Sir
N. Plunkett, "as persons in all respects worthy and
answerable to that employment, in order to obtain
from Innocent X. assistance for the Confederates".
He returned home, Nov., 1648, landed at Waterford,
and proceeded thence to Kilkenny, where he found
the position of the Catholics sadly changed for the
worse since his departure. He now saw O'Neill and
the Nuncio party defeated, the Nuncio himself driven
to Connaught, Inchiquin's army declaring for the
King, Ormonde feasting at ease in his own castle at
Kilkenny, and the general assembly ready to ratify
a second peace. He explained in person the result
of his embassy before the council, and sent a report
of his address to the Nuncio. There can be no doubt
that in this crisis he despaired of the confederate
cause, and that his unfavourable account hastened
the peace by discouraging the adverse party. His
own readiness to accept the terms was enough to
daunt less firm councillors.

After the peace he was one of the twelve commissioners appointed to see that the Lord Lieu-

tenant should carry out faithfully the articles of the treaty.

He and his friend Sir N. Plunkett were deputed by Ormonde to treat with Owen Roe O'Neill, and succeeded in bringing that chieftain and the whole northern army over to the royal party.

In the meanwhile Cromwell's army was desolating all the important towns, and levelling the strongest fortresses. The royalists blamed Ormonde for their disasters, and even the bishops in their solemn synod at Jamestown, in Aug. 1650, condemned him as the author of all the misfortunes that followed the peace. In 1651 Dr. French was commissioned by the Catholic leaders to seek assistance from the Duke of Lorraine; but though that prince showed every disposition to advance their cause, he had neither men nor money. This embassy also failing, there remained no further hope at home or abroad. The country was swept from sea to sea by the Cromwellian soldiers, and the Catholic prelates and priests were all banished from the kingdom. It seems certain that Dr. French did not return to Ireland after 1651, nor visit his diocese ever after the fall of Wexford in 1649. An interesting account of his escape is contained in the subjoined documents, the first of which was never before published.

Ea quae D.V. Illma. dixit Domino Cleary, urbana, benigna, amantia, grandem, quam semper habui, de magnitudine animi tui, ac constantia, de candore ac speciali in me immeritum affectu, plenissime confirmarunt opinionem. Sed quare, Mi Dne. Illme., quidam in urbe, qui sensu suo abundant et meum ignorant, judicant me trepidum, et quasi expallescentem ad calamitates, quas debeo experire, et eas sic formidantem, quod videar commoditates, quibus fruor, anteferre solicitudini et amori gregis dilectissimi? Scio tamen abundare, et scio egere: parvi facio regulas hujus mundi cito advolantis, et conabor cum Paulo dicere: sive vivimus sive morimur, Dni sumus, ejus volo esse in æternum.

Fateor cum ingenti animæ gratitudine Emos. Dnos. meos de Propda. majorem mihi exhibuisse munificentiam, quam aliis Præsulibus, quod mihi (sic existimo) debebatur qui plus aliis passus sum, et una die pro Deo et fide (quod nulli fralium meorum contigit) omnia amisi, nempe. 11 Octobr. an. 1649. Illa funestissima die civitas Wexfordia, gentilitia, opibus, ratibus, mercimoniis florens, in ore gladii deleta fuit, et furenti militi in prædam data a Cromvello peste imperii Anglicani: ceciderunt ante altare Dei victimæ sacræ sancti Dni sacerdotes, alii extra fores templi reperti flagellis cæsi sunt, alii capti et vincti catenis, alii suspensi, alii crudeliter necati.] Fundebatur clarus civium sanguis quo inundabant plateæ, vix erat domus non fœdata sanguine, et plena ploratu. In ipso palatio immaniter trucidati sunt unus ephoebus, amabilis puer, hortulanus, et sacristanus, capellanum vero, quem domi reliqueram sex gravibus vulneribus affectum, reliquerunt in cruore suo volutatum. Et hæc abominanda facta sunt in facie solis a profanis sicariis, a qua die non vidi (quod me facit hominem sub sole miserrimum) civitatem, gregem, patriam, gentem. A civitatis excidio vixi in sylvis 5 mensibus, in horas ad necem quæsitus. Ibi erat potus meus lac et aqua, panis in arcta mensura, quem quidem semel spatio 5 dierum non gustavi. cibus nulla arte coquorum conditus. Cubavi sub dio sine lecto et stragulis. Demum sylva in qua delitui, densis hostium turmis circumdata, qui eo venerant, ut me caperent et in Angliam mitterent catenis ligatum, erupi angelo tutelari me ducente, ac evasi generosi equi velocitate.

Iam peto a gratia tua, an tam acerba passus pro Deo et religione non habeam jus ad aliquam portionem panis ac patrimonii Jesu Chi? an forte negabit probato militi Chi opem et stipendium Dux supremus ecclesiæ militantis Ssmus. D. P. Clemens X.? et dedit et dabit auxilium presuli septuagenario sub purpureo crucis vexillo militanti.

Haec sunt quæ duxi scribenda D.V. Illmæ. die 9 Jan., 1673.

"All that your Excellency said to Mr. Cleary shows your

politeness, affection, and goodness, and confirms the opinion
that I always entertained of your magnanimity, constancy, and
sincerity, and of your special regard for me, though unworthy
of your favour. But why, my Lord, do some persons in Rome,
who know their own motives, and know not my position,
charge me with timidity, and describe me as pale with fear at
the thought of the calamities which I should manfully meet,
and through which fear I shun all danger, it seems, preferring
my own ease and comfort to the care and love which I owe
to my flock? I know, however, both how to abound and to
suffer need. I make little account of the maxims of this fleet-
ing world, and I shall strive to say with Paul, ' Whether we
live or whether we die, we are the Lord's'. I wish to be His
for ever. I confess, most gratefully, that their Eminences of the
Propaganda were more generous to me than to other bishops,
perhaps because I suffered more than others, for I lost in one
day, namely, the 11th of October, 1649, for my God and my
religion (what happened to no one else), all that I had in the
world. On that most unhappy day, the town of Wexford,
the home of my family, abounding in wealth, shipping, and
commerce, was taken at the point of the sword and given up
for plunder to a furious soldiery by Cromwell, the worst plague
of English dominion in Ireland. On that day there fell before the altar of God, as sacred victims, the holy priests of the
Lord; some when found outside the porch of the church were
flogged to death, some were taken and bound with chains,
others hanged, and others cruelly murdered. The streets
flowed with the noble blood of the citizens. There was hardly
a house that was not stained with gore and filled with wailing.
In the episcopal palace were cruelly slain a beautiful youth,
the gardener, and the sacristan. The chaplain, who remained
there by my orders, they left covered with blood, having inflicted on him six mortal wounds. And these detestable
crimes were perpetrated in the open day by impious assassins.
From that day to this I never saw (which makes me the most
pitiable of men) my family town, my flock, my country, or my
kindred. After the fall of Wexford I wandered for five months
through the woods, hunted every hour by those who sought
my death. During that time my drink was milk and water;

my only food bread in scanty measure; and even this I did not taste on one occasion for five days. I used no cooked food at all. I slept in the open air without bed or covering. At length, when the wood in which I lay concealed was surrounded by a large force of the enemy, who came to arrest me in order to send me in chains to England, I escaped through the protection of my guardian angel and the swiftness of my good horse.

I now ask your Grace, whether I, who have suffered so much for my God and for my faith, am not entitled to some portion of the patrimony of Jesus Christ for my maintenance? Can the supreme ruler of the Church militant, our most holy Father Clement the Tenth, deny a little aid and a pension to a soldier who has served so faithfully? No, he will give, as he has given hitherto, assistance to a prelate now seventy years of age, who has fought well under the purple banner of the cross. This account I thought proper to lay before your Excellency, on this 9th day of January, 1673".

The other document (preserved in T.C.D. Library) is quoted by the Rev. Mr. Meehan in a letter to the *Wexford People*, from which we take this extract. Dr. French, refuting the false account of the state of Ireland given by an opponent, addresses him thus:

"You say nothing of Wexford, cruelly carried at the point of the sword on the 11th of October; nothing of my plundered palace or household therein;* nothing of my priests, precious victims, immolated before the altar by the swords of impious heretics; nothing of the brave citizens weltering in their blood. I was lying sick of a burning fever in a town hard by. From that day forward I never saw my beloved town or the face of my people. I became an outcast, fleeing into the deserted country. For five months I wandered through forests and mountains that I might solace the remnant of my flock saved from the common slaughter. They had also fled to the fastnesses for protection".

* The Bishop's house, or rather its site, is still pointed out by tradition.

His papers, he adds, showing his loyalty to the king, fell into Cromwell's hands, and provoked him to more bitter hatred of the Catholics.

After the bootless visit to the Duke of Lorraine, as there was no possible chance of returning to Ireland, Dr. French proceeded first to Paris, in the hope of seeing Charles II.; but the king, advised by Ormonde, refused an audience. Thence he went to Spain about the close of 1652, and there laboured as coadjutor archbishop of St. Iago until 1666. He enjoyed a liberal provision, and during his stay in Gallicia, had perhaps more temporal comfort than he could expect in Ireland in the best of times. Still he felt unhappy and lonely in exile, and ardently longed to see his beloved flock. Towards the close of 1666 he received a letter from the famous Peter Walsh, the schismatical friar, the devoted creature of Ormonde, inviting him home, and promising protection, no doubt in the hope that the bishop would favour the Remonstrance. But the scheme did not succeed. Dr. French resigned, it is true, his pension and place in Gallicia, and set out forthwith for Ireland ; but lest his acceptance of the invitation should be misinterpreted as a pledge of his support to the wily Walsh, he wrote to Ormonde, explaining his views on the question of the Remonstrance.

MAY IT PLEASE YOUR GRACE,

A friend from them parts advised me to write a submissive, humble letter, begging pardon of your Grace, and that after such a letter nothing would remain to obstruct my going home, and your Grace's protecting me hereafter [offers an apology in general terms]. . . . To come nearer the point, as a Christian I may not deny a rational satisfaction even to the meanest person injured by me. That being so, the question is, what is the crime I should seek pardon for, how great, and when committed against your Grace? For what hath passed before the peace (if not murder or some black doings of which I am not guilty) the act of oblivion giveth me and all a pardon and safety. Since the peace I have faithfully observed the articles thereof, and never betrayed the common interest. There is not any man living can accuse me in that way. But the doings of Jamestown [where he signed against Ormonde] are objected as treasonable, a breach of the pacification, and a pulling down of kingly authority in the interest of the nation. The message the Bishop of Dromore and Dr. Kelly, Dean of Tuam, brought from the prelates to your Excellency, maketh this manifest, in what a lamentable condition the country was then, how little those faithful to the king had, being driven all of us into a corner of one province; how unlike we were to recover what was lost, or defend what we held, no man knoweth better than your Grace. The king was also then in the hands of the Scottish Presbyterians, deadly enemies to the Catholics of Ireland, so as there was no access to his Majesty. In the opinion of all there was need of a speedy cure for the nation in danger, or all was given for lost. The prelates that met at Jamestown had some months before in the congregation of Clonmacnois (as your Grace knoweth well) coöperated to the best of their power with your Excellency, and made ordinances for keeping the people in obedience under his Majesty, and in union with one another under your government; for there was fear the enemy, then powerful, would debauch them from their duty. Our thoughts in Jamestown were the same we had in Clonmacnois, and all of us aimed at the safety of all interests, and represented as we then conceived to your Excellency the right expedient of settling all things the best way the times did then permit. If we did not hit the remedy, we had a good mind to do so without any man's prejudice. . . If I shall say about the doings of Jamestown other than what I have said, which is the true dictamen of my soul, I shall belie myself and betray my fame, which is a sin before God. Yet for all this, I had rather in this particular, and all others of this kind, depend upon his Majesty's clemency and your Grace's benignity, than mine innocency.

After an apology for some pieces he wrote in Paris against Ormonde, which he says were severe, but written under great provocation from others, he adds:

Having ingenuously confessed all I could say against myself, I have reason to expect your Grace's pardon and protection, which I pray may be signified unto me by some of your trusty secretaries, that I may know the waters of your anger are fallen. My lord, where I am, I am well looked upon, and enjoy a subsistence competent and decent for quality; whereas going home I had nothing before me for relieving me, my church and lands being transferred to another hand; most of all my friends are dead and gone; a few worthy gentlemen allied to me (who have a willingness to subsist me) live themselves in poverty, and in great fear they will not be restored to their own. Notwithstanding all these incommodities, if my weak forces (for I am afflicted with many sharp pangs of infirmity) will serve me, and that I may enjoy your Grace's protection for discharging a trust God put upon me, I am resolved to set forward. Were it not for this reason of duty to God, and love to my flock, your Grace may confidently believe my exile would be more pleasing than my country. God prosper and protect your Grace (for which I have now for some years heartily prayed); so wishing, with a submissive kiss of your hand, my lord, your Grace's most obedient and humble servant,

NICS. FERNENSIS.*

In a letter to P. Walsh of the same date, the bishop writes:

. . . His Excellency will find me as trusty as any of the king's own bishops. I bring not with me the spirit of dependence or ambition. I aim not at worldly honours or commodities (for I enjoy more here than I can there); that I seek after (God is my witness) is only and solely my dear lambs and flock (their fleece and milk are in another hand: if he will content himself with both and seek not to vex me, I will be

* Walsh's *Rem.*, pp. 618-630.

patient with the lack of both), and to give a right account to
God of the sacred *depositum*, the charge of souls committed by
Him to my trust and care, which commission can hardly be
discharged by me without some toleration and liberty. Both
I may in some measure enjoy supported by his Grace's protection. . . . But if it shall come to that extremity [leave to
return being refused], what is to be done? In my opinion it
would be the resolution of a languishing spirit, if the fear of
men in such circumstances would be able to deter a bishop
from doing the work of God, and attending his flock. If I am
put to it in this matter, I conceive my best answer will be that
of the Apostles, "*obedire oportet Deo magis quam homini*".

A friend, named Archbold, brought these two
letters to P. Walsh, who gave them to Ormonde, and
in two months after, March 10, 1666, wrote this
most impudent letter:

"You must", he says to the bishop, "write a more submissive letter as to Jamestown affairs, and such other public
actings in former times here, and write the total change of
your judgment in reference to all such matters".

And again,

I will advise your Lordship not to venture any further than
Paris or Louvain, or some near place on that side the sea, until
I send to you again, after you have altered your style on the
above subjects. . . . You may come without danger to
yourself or others, if you please to do what, by the law of
Christ, you may and ought to do, viz., confess you have done
ill, crave his Majesty's pardon, and assure him under your
hand *by the same instrument* we have [the Remonstrance] of
your future fidelity towards him. . . . Again I return to
yourself and the duke. He thinks you a good man, good
priest, and good bishop. And thinks you candid and without
cheat. And he knows you would (if your understanding in
that one matter were rightly principled) be of more use both
as to parts and feeling, than many others of your calling and
dignity. There is a general congregation to be held in

Dublin the 11th of June next. You may be there if you leave Spain in time, *and if you return in time to this such other letters as become you.* For *then*, I shall send you the duke's license, *otherwise not.* This goes to you by the way of Paris and my Lord of Armagh. I am, with all my soul, your most affectionate and humble servant, P. WALSH.

From the letter to Ormonde, it was perfectly plain that Dr. French would never approve the Remonstrance. Walsh's reply was sent off immediately, but did not reach the bishop until he came to St. Sebastian, on his way home, not doubting but that the protection so solemnly promised would be vouchsafed to him. On the 10th of May, 1666, the day after receiving Walsh's answer, the bishop wrote again, saying:

My will, you may be well assured, doth not stick to write anything may give satisfaction to the King and Duke, that my conscience can agree unto; yea, and to change my understanding as to the actings past and as to the future, if you will give reasons strong enough for making such a change; but I have consulted many learned divines, who all tell me I cannot change. I have now quitted my settlement in Gallicia, much to the grief of my lord archbishop, and I am now thinking to put myself as near home as I can, until God will be pleased to give an end of this difficulty (Walsh's *Rem.*, p. 624).

From St. Sebastian, Dr. French travelled on to Paris, whence he wrote thus to Walsh, Paris, July 18, 1666:

FATHER WALSH,
I hope you had ere this my answer from St. Sebastian, of the 10th of May, to yours of the 11th of March, sent away by a little Spanish vessel. I had adventured over with the same, but for your letter, which, had it overtaken me in St. Iago's, I had not come to France. By the said answer, I briefly told you that I have for my opinion against yours, touching some

tenets of the Protestation, seven saints, and St. Thomas one of them, seven cardinals, one patriarch, three archbishops, ten bishops, and thirty-one classical authors, with other eminent divines. All of these were persons of great learning and authority, and good and faithful subjects, and taught others to be so. I wonder, then, how you would have me forsake such grave and learned sages, or say my understanding is ill-principled, following these men.

Seeing the Duke is satisfied (as you write) for anything done at Paris, and that he thinks I am a good man, good priest, good bishop, candid and without cheat, and yet will not have me come to my country; and in the meantime calleth Ardmach home, of whom he had not so good an opinion, I know not what to say, but must tell you this is a mystery all that hear thereof wonder at, and none can penetrate or understand it. I say not this envying that afflicted man this happiness, if he will find it to be so.

After the great heats we have here, I intend to give reasons more at large why I may not with quietness of mind sign the Protestation, as the Duke and you demand (at the more substantial parts thereof I do not scruple or stagger). I will also answer some parts of your letter, which intrencheth this much upon me. . . . And seeing for aught to me appearing, I cannot satisfy my conscience and the duke together, nor become profitable to my flock at home, nor live quietly and secure, his anger not being appeased, you may know hereby that I am resolved after dog days to go to Lonvain, and there end my days where I began my studies. I shall thereby free you from giving further trouble to the Duke in mediating for me, and give myself a freedom from many personal afflictions and troubles good men endure there, though my heart shall still have a share in their sufferings. Do me the friendship and right of showing this letter to the Duke, and send your answer to this city, in the form beneath written. God grant a blessing of peace and tranquillity upon that nation; and even so, I remain, sir, your affectionate servant,

NICS. FERNENSIS.*

*Remons., p. 625.

For about two years Dr. French remained in Paris, acting in the meantime as coadjutor to his Eminence Cardinal John F. de Goudy, by whom he had been most graciously received, and hoping still to get a more favourable opportunity of returning to Ireland. But when at length it became manifest that there was but little chance of a speedy end of the long and fierce struggle raging there, Dr. French withdrew to Flanders, wishing to revisit the scenes of his early years, perhaps to seek the advice and aid of his college friends, and to end his days where he began his studies. On his way to Louvain he stopped at Ghent, where he was employed as coadjutor by the bishop of that see, M. Eugene Albert de Allamont, till the 23rd of August, 1678, the day on which he resigned his pure spirit into the hands of God. His remains were buried with solemn rite before the great altar of the parochial church of St. Nicholas. Over them is placed a white marble monument, with his arms and truthful motto "virtus in angustiis" engraved, bearing the inscription, which we copy (*infra*) from the *Hib. Dom.*, p. 490. In the dearth of native testimony, it often happens that we find among foreign writers the fullest and most interesting notices of distinguished Irishmen. Few readers will imagine that many particulars to which we have referred in Dr. French's life—are gleaned from a book, entitled *Histoire des Eveques*, etc., *de S. Bavon* a Gand (in two vols. 8vo, Gand, 1772).

During his residence in Ghent, Dr. French frequently visited the Internuncio at Brussels to consult with him on Irish ecclesiastical affairs. He also wrote many letters to P. Walsh to bring him to a sense of duty, and to procure his reconciliation to the

Church. The short intervals of leisure which holier duties left at his disposal, he employed in vindicating the faith of the Irish Catholic people, and their policy in the war of 1641, being, as he says, in 1673, when he wrote some of his works, the only survivor among the bishops "of all the excommunicated peace-breakers". The following is a list of the books, which Dr. French acknowledged to be genuine in his correspondence with Walsh. 1. A *Narrative* of the Sale and Settlement of Ireland, Louvain, 1668, 4to. 2. *Lucubrationes* Episcopi Fernensis in Hispania. 3. A Latin piece, entitled "*Neque Praescripsit*". 4. 30 Sheets of Reasons for not subscribing the Remonstrance. 5. *A synopsis* justifying the War. 6. *Religion in England* with the due obedience of Catholics annexed. 7. The *Bleeding Iphigenia*, "being", says Walsh, "a portraiture of Ireland, and intended by him as a forerunner to a greater work against the Acts of Settlement of that kingdom since the Restoration". 8. The *Unkind Deserter of Loyal Men and True Friends*. These two books were reprinted by Mr. Duffy under the skilful editorial care of the Rev. Mr. Meehan. 9. The *Doleful Fall of Andrew Sall*, by N. F., 8vo, 1675. This Sall was a Jesuit, but not the superior (I believe) of that order in Cashel. In Verdier's Report, 20th June, 1649, he was said to be 33 years old, and teaching school in Clonmel; after his apostacy he was honoured with the degree of D.D. in Dublin University, went to London, where he was caressed by some of those lords, like the Earl of Orrery, who are the ever ready and pious patrons of schismatical or suspected priests. Sall was the worst preacher of his order in Ireland, and yet his eloquence and unction attracted crowded and fashionable audiences in the English churches. Dr. French knew him in early life, grieved heartily for his doleful fall, and wrote this book to bring about his conversion, and to remove the evil effects of his scandalous example. Others also refuted Sall, who in 1676, after his return to Dublin, published a reply to three of them—viz., J. S. (John Sargeant, an English priest), J. E., and N. N. Though Dr. French was the first to denounce Sall, and well known to him from the beginning, and though Sall expressly promised in his published reply to others, to answer the bishop's pamphlet also, he never did, moved, we may hope, by reverence and gratitude. Walsh's Four Letters *passim*.

Dr. French passed to a better world on 23rd Aug., 1678. The inscription on his monument limits his episcopate to *thirty* years. It seems strange that De Burgo, who gives the epitaph, and (relying on the authority of Harris) the date of accession as sixteen hundred and *forty-three*, does not advert to the discrepancy. But even if we reject the early date of consecration, and put it back to 1645, as we have done, Dr. French would have been bishop of Ferns nearly thirty-three years.

D. O. M.
Siste, viator, audi, lege, luge.
Iacet hic illustrissimus ac Piissimus Praesul,
Nicolaus French,
Fernensium in Hibernia episcopus humilis,
sacrae Pontificiae capellae comes assistens,
Supremi consilii regni Hiberniae consiliarius,
ab eodem ad Innocentium X. Papam
cum auctoritate deputatus.
Illustrissimorum ac R. R. Episcoporum
In Gallicia, Parisiensis in Gallia, ac demum Gandavensis
in Flandria-coadjutor indefessus, haeresiarcharum

ac haereticorum tam verbo quam calamo profligator acerrimus, collegii pastoralis Hibernorum Lovanii alumnus, magister, praeses, benefactor, fundata ibidem bursa 180 Florenorum annuatim in perpetuum pro capacioribus ingeniis; tandem exulatus sui dilectis patria, episcopatu, et grege ob fidem annos 25 praesul emeritus, emensis pro ecclesia Deo innumeris periculis, ac persecutionibus, cunctis semper gratus, omnibus spectabilis, non sine magno Patriae suae praejudicio, bonorumque suspiriis, ac lachrymis, hoc marmore tegitur, qui vere fuit animo Pontifex, verbo angelus, vita sacerdos.

Obiit Gandavi in metropoli Flandriae, aetatis anno 74, Episcopatus 30, Incarnationis Dominicae 1678, mensis Augusti die vigesima tertia.

LUKE WADDING, cons. 1672; ob. 1688.

According to an old tradition among the faithful of Ferns, Luke Wadding, their bishop, was nephew of the celebrated Franciscan historian of that name, but a native of Wexford, where the Waddings flourished for many a generation; their chief stronghold being Wadding's castle, in the parish of St. Patrick, town of Wexford. The bishop was descended from, if not the son of, John Wadding, of Ballycogly, county Wexford. Harris says " he was born (*I think*) in the county Wexford, was titular bishop of Ferns, a Doctor of the Sorbonne, a secular priest; and buried in the Franciscan convent of Wexford. He published in the reign of Charles II. '*A small garland* of pious and godly songs for the solace of his friends and neighbours.'" This Garland had passed through many editions, but that which Harris saw was in 12mo, published in London, 1731, Ware's Irish Writers, p. 139. I saw this day, Oct. 2,

1840, another edition, London, 1728, the editor of which says he again published it because its poems, intended chiefly for the consolation of persons suffering for religion, were as necessary in his day as in those of the good bishop who wrote them, and was long since beyond the reach of earthly punishment for so meritorious a work. Among the poems I noticed one on the Christmas day of 1687, in which the writer says there was no Mass allowed, and suggests that another name should be given to that day, for it was not in truth a *Christ's-mass*. From lines inserted in another poem it is plain that it was written in prison, where the bishop had been detained for a long time under sentence of banishment *now a second time*, for he had been already banished under Cromwell. But in that exile he felt himself more happy than at home, because he was with his lawful king, Charles II. Now, he was to leave his country, perhaps for ever, on account of his faith, and the sad day, the 20th of Nov. following, was not far distant. He should still suffer cheerfully, and hope for a better future. In all the poems, the thoughts are instructive and pious, but the language and versification merit no special praise.

Dr. Wadding was P.P. of New Ross, and Vicar-General of Ferns during the exile of Dr. French, at whose urgent request he was appointed coadjutor bishop in 1672, with right of succession. Up to that time Dr. French thought that he might be permitted to return to his diocese, but when the letters of Walsh precluded all further hope, he recommended Dr. Wadding as his successor. The following document, first published in the Dublin *Evening*

News, of Feb 7, 1860, the original of which is preserved in the archives of the Propaganda, shows the feelings with which the good priest received the unwelcome tidings of his own promotion :

ILLUSTRISSIME DOMINE,—Accipe summarium eorum, quæ hodie per aliam viam destinavi. Cum vestris quamplures recepi inclusas ad D. Norton, simulque literas Illustrissimi D. Internuncii cum iis quæ mihi ex parte S. Congnis. de Propaganda transmissæ sunt, quibus omnibus devictus, me tandem resigno, ut voluntati vestræ obsecundem, quantum per vires et capacitatem licuerit, etsi propter dispositionem præsentem nostratum, propter extremam inopiam omnium hic, temporis incertitudinem, innumerasque rationes, vere ad hoc minus propensus.

Distuli consecrationem, quamvis a Dublinens, consultus, ut fieret per Cassel. Ossorien. et Waterford. donec videro an adhuc forte spes aliqua effulgeat desideratam videndi faciem vestram. Expendi quæcumque mecum contuli, nullum enim hic sublevamen habui nisi a solis illis duabus familiis, olim suæ Illustrissimæ Dom. notis, quarum una hinc jam migravit, eruntque modo omnes, ut mihi subveniant tepidiores, si munus tam publicum, suscipiam; cujus quippe causa ne incommodum patiantur, merito verebuntur, quibus omnibus bene perpensis, debeo mihi de necessariis prospicere, cum tamen nec habeam, quo vel famulum, vel alium quemcumque sustineam. Pontificale, mitra, pedum, pectorale, annulus, et quæcunque ad Episcopum spectant, mihi desunt, nec ullum video modum acquirendi; propter hæc et alias extremitates, gloriari poterit coadjutor vester se tam pauperem esse, ac quondam fuere piscatores, dum ad hominum vocarentur piscationem: advisamentum vestrum ac mandata prestolabor. Anne potituri sumus consolatione desideratæ præsentiæ vestræ, vota sunt D. D. Norton, et Rossitter. Pauca jam scribo ad illustrissimum Dominum Internuncium, sed supplebit solita benignitate S. D. Illustrissimus defectum. Pauperimus Episcopus, clerus et populus toto orbe pauperior, opprimor Epistolis, aliisque curis. Quamdiu sic subsistam plane ignoro; hoc unicum mihi solatii est, quod mera obedientia ad hanc capessendam dignitatem compellor." Paternus vester erga natale solum affectus ac opinio, quam plane supra meritum de me concepit, munus tam impar meritis, quam longe a votis super me attraxit. Spem quamdam domum repetendi nobis præbes; alii contrarium persuadent. Anhelo ad vestram resolutionem tam pro tuorum consolatione, quam adversariorum confusione. Si tandem hoc munus suscipiam Domino Norton de præsenti quo fungar prospiciendum est, quem capaciorem judico. In ambitione ad dignitates mecum plane convenit. A paschate cum Dei adjutorio propensiones meas omnes conferam, ut desiderio vestro, et Apostolicis mandatis satisfaciam, et vere hoc potius ex mera obedientia, ac veneratione ad ea, quæ transmissa sunt. Altissimus abunde remuneraturus est paternam quam habes hujus loci curam, et alia quæcumque fecisti pro filiis domi forisque. Nomen vestrum ac memoria in veneratione apud omnes hic habentur, quæ non mediocris est consolatio iis qui te diligunt; inter quos me primo ordine collocabo, qui ex toto corde optarem me nunquam a vobis ita fuisse dilectum, ut me ad tale munus eveheres, de quo nunquam vel minima mihi incidit cogitatio. In dies singulos quatuor quinqueve literas scribo, præter alia, quæ quotidie sunt peragenda. Non mediocris mihi foret solatii, si vel famulum retinere possem. Hactenus me sustinui proprio marte et quorumdam amicorum adjutorio, qui, ut experior, in dies decrescunt ac tepescunt. Ut video sum mansurus idem, et, ut conjicio ad pejora perferenda procinctus. Rogo ut præsenti hac occasione scribas; si pectorale vobis superfluat, dignabitur mittere; annulum bene hic procurabo, mittas etiam mitram, pedum, et omnes vestes violaceas cum omnibus ad missam Pontificalem necessariis, nam nulla hic habenda est. Si ipse in persona poterit venire, est summum quod omnes expectamus et specialiter.—Vester,

Lucas Waddingus.

Rossoponti, 1 Feb., 1672.

Most Illustrious Lord,—Accept a summary of the information which I have forwarded to you this day by another route. With yours I have received the several enclosures to Mr. Norton—the letters of the Internuncio, and likewise those which were transmitted to me by the Sacred Congregation de Propaganda. Overpowered by these communications, I resign myself in order that I may conform to your will as far as my strength and ability will allow; though, indeed, on account of the actual condition of our people, the extreme poverty of all here, the uncertainty of the times, and other numerous reasons, I am very little disposed to take upon me an office of such responsibility.

I have postponed the consecration (although advised by the Archbishop of Dublin that it should be performed by the Archbishop of Cashel and the Bishops of Ossory and Waterford) till I shall have learned whether there is still any hope of beholding your beloved person here. I have already laid out all that I brought with me to this place, for indeed I have had no means of support in this quarter save what I received from the two families formerly well known to your lordship; one of them has already emigrated, and, as for those who remain, they all will grow lukewarm if I accept such a conspicuous dignity; for they justly dread that it may expose them to greater losses. Having seriously considered all this, it behoves me to provide myself with necessaries, for I am so poor that I cannot support a servant, or indeed any one else. I want a Pontifical, a Mitre, Pastoral Staff, Pectoral Cross, and Ring, for I lack all that a bishop requires, nor do I see any way of procuring them here. By reason of these and other extremities, your coadjutor can boast that he is as poor as formerly were the fishermen when they were called to the fishing of men. I am anxiously awaiting your advice and commands. Messrs. Norton and Rossitter are constantly asking shall we ever again enjoy the consolation of your longed-for presence? I send a few lines to the Internuncio, but your lordship, with your wonted kindness, will supply my shortcomings. The poorest of bishops, with a clergy equally poor, and a flock than which the world has not poorer, I am overwhelmed with correspondence and other cares.

I cannot conjecture how long I may be able to exist in this state, but my only consolation is that I am compelled by mere obedience to take this dignity on me. Your paternal love of native land, and the estimate you have formed of me—so far transcending any merits of mine—have induced you to select me for an office which is as incompatible with my deserts as it is farthest from my wishes. You give us some hope of returning home; others, however, think differently. I am very anxious to ascertain what you mean to do, and this as much for the comfort of your friends as for the confounding of your enemies. If I eventually accept this dignity, I think that Mr. Norton should be preferred to the office which I now hold, for I am convinced that he is the fittest for it. As for ambitioning dignities, his views are entirely in accordance with mine.

After Easter, with God's help, I will make you aware of my final resolve, in order to satisfy your wishes and the Apostolic mandates, simply through mere obedience and veneration for the orders which have been transmitted to me. The Most High will one day reward you for the paternal care of this place, and also for all that you have done for its children, both at home and abroad. Your name and memory are held in veneration by all here, and this is no small consolation to those who love you, among whom I would fain hold the first place; though in sooth I wish from my heart I had never been so beloved by you as that you would have thought me worthy of being elevated to such a dignity, the faintest dream of which never crossed my mind. I am obliged to write four or five letters every day, besides attending to the ordinary routine duties. It would be a great comfort to me if I had the means of supporting a servant. Up to the present I have existed on my own resources and the assistance given me by few a friends, who, I perceive, are daily decreasing and growing lukewarm. As far as I can see, I believe that I am destined to continue in the same state, nay, and to be prepared for worse. I beseech you to write to me by the present opportunity. If you can spare a Pectoral Cross, have the kindness to send it to me. I can easily procure a Ring here. Send me the Mitre, the Crozier, and all the violet Vestments, with everything else necessary for a Pontifical Mass, for nothing of the sort can be had here. If yourself can come in person, it will be the crowning of all our desires, and especially of those of your

LUKE WADDING.

Ross, 1st Feb., 1672.

Dr. Wadding was one of the Irish bishops to whom James II., on March, 1685, ordered a pension of

£150 a year to be paid. On the 24th July, same year, he assisted at the Provincial Council held in Dublin, with his vicar-general and successor in the see, Michael Rossiter. Among the papers at St. Isidore's, may be seen an interesting collection of testimonials from Irish bishops in favour of the Franciscans, from which the following signatures are taken, with their respective dates:

Datum e loco refugii nostri, die 30 Jan., 1684.
  Fr. Patricius Clogher, Administrator Kilmor.
  Dominicus Armacanus, 22 Feb., 1684.
  Patric. Dublinensis, 2 Mar., 1685.
  Fr. Dominicus Elphinensis, 27 Feb., 1684.
  Jacobus Lynceus, Abbas de Conga, 8 Feb., 1684.
  Jacobus Ossoriensis, 12 Mar., 1684.
  Lucas Fernensis, 21 Mar., 1684.
  Joan. De Burgo, Canonicus Tuamensis, 15 Mar., 1684.

In the letter (Paris, Oct. 28, 1692) of Archbishop James Lynch, of Tuam, to the Cardinal Perfect of Propaganda, there is a feeling notice of Dr. Wadding's trials towards the end of his life:

"The Bishop of Ferns, after the fall of Wexford, and its subjection to the enemies of our faith, fled to Connaught, and we both lived together until the subversion of our province. We then went to Limerick and bore all the hardships of our camp. After the taking of Limerick he returned to his wretched flock, which was reduced to the utmost want, desiring to hide himself there if possible, in order to exercise among them his pastoral duty as far as he could. But in a short time afterwards his life of hardships received there a glorious end. He was a truly distinguished man, a pious and most vigilant pastor."—Theiner MSS.

Dr. Wadding died in 1688—not in 1687 (*Hib. Dom.* p. 815) as is plain from the Garland—and was buried in the chapel yard of Wexford. Over his remains is laid a horizontal slab on a level with the surface of the earth. The inscription, which I am credibly informed could be easily read within the early part of this century, and was read by some men yet living, as I learned from the best authority, is now entirely effaced, the slab being in the very centre of the pathway to the old parish chapel.

MICHAEL ROSSITER, *suc.* 1693; *ob.* 1709.

It has been assumed, perhaps too hastily, that Michael Rossiter (Rausiter or Raucetter, for the name is spelled differently in old records), bishop of Ferns, is the same person who returned himself in the government register of 1704, as 56 years of age, parish priest of Killenick, and ordained Dec. 27, 1672, in Lisbon, by the Most Rev. Gabriel de Almeida, bishop of Funchall. The fact may be so, but it should not be taken for granted, for these reasons. It is quite certain that Dr. Rossiter was appointed bishop of Ferns long before 1704. He was nominated by James II. on the 3rd Nov., 1692 (Bodleian Papers, D. N. n. 25), and was probably appointed to the see of Ferns the next year. The bishop of Ferns is named expressly among the four prelates who were supposed to be in Ireland, in the return drawn up by the Bishop of Ossory, which was presented to the Nuncio at Paris, July, 1698. (Theiner MSS). He was therefore bishop when the government census was taken. That he might still have described himself as P.P. cannot be denied, for it was not unusual for bishops to pass as parish priests, or even as medical doctors, to escape detection; but we find no other contemporary bishop registered as P.P., and the name of Rossiter was, and is still, common in Wexford. It seems difficult, therefore, to decide whether the bishop is the person named in the government return. We have seen already that Michael Rossiter assisted at the Provincial Council of Dublin, July 24, 1685, in the acts of which he is described as "vicar-general of Ferns, representing the chapter of that diocese". He was dean in 1692 when recommended by James II.

Of Dr. Rossiter's manner of life after his consecration, very little seems to be known. His name is not even mentioned by any of the Irish writers except De Burgo, who merely tells us that he succeeded Wadding, and died in 1709 (*Hib. Dom.*, p. 815).

JOHN VERDON, *suc.* 1704; *ob.* 1728.

John Verdon was a native of Louth, a student of the College of Lisbon, and parish priest of St. Peter's, Drogheda. In the registry of 1704 he appears as parish priest of St. Peter's, Drogheda, having been ordained at Lisbon in 1687, and being at the time of registration (1703) 41 years of age.

Before his promotion to the see of Ferns he had been Vicar-General of Armagh. The letter of James II., recommending him for the bishopric, still extant, gives a summary of his life:

> Joannem Verdun e clero seculari, S.T.D., et Vicarium Generalem dioecesis Armacanae, virum magnae pietatis, prudentiae et zeli, multisque sane annis in vinea Domini cum fructu laborantem, populo ac clero imprimis gratum, nominavimus ad Episcopatum Fernensem in Lageniensi provincia, in qua non est alius episcopus nisi Dublinensis (Theiner MSS.).

Dr. Verdon was consecrated Bishop of Ferns at the close of 1709, but I know not the exact date. Among the diocesan papers in the hands of the late Most Rev. Dr. Keating, there was a very curious document authenticating a relic of the holy cross, brought from Rome for the use of the cathedral church by Dr. French, and kept after Cromwell's time in the family of Colonel Butler, whose deposition is witnessed to by Dr. Verdon, June 14, 1716. See these declarations in *Record*, vol. viii. p. 256. Another document respecting the foundations of Dr. French in foreign colleges, said to be signed by Dr. Verdon, if it ever existed, is no longer to be found in the archives of Ferns.

Some annoyance was caused to Dr. Verdon by a dispute regarding the collation of a benefice. It was alleged that he did not appoint to the parish within six months after the vacancy, and that consequently, according to the rule of the Chancellory, his power to collate had expired. Acting on this statement, the Archbishop of Dublin appointed the Rev. Mr. Redmond to the benefice; but Dr. Verdon proved clearly that another priest had been not only named, but publicly inducted by him within the six months allowed by the canons. Redmond's nomination was therefore declared null and void by the Primate of Armagh, who was appealed to to settle the dispute. *Jus. Prim. Armac*, p. 10. Of the progress of religion in Ferns, while Dr. Verdon governed the see, we have strong evidence in the report of the Lords' committee, appointed to inquire into the state of Popery in Ireland in 1730. It sets forth that in the diocese of Ferns there were then "21 old Mass houses, and *ten built since the accession of George I.* (A.D. 1714), besides three private chapels, 44 officiating priests, and two friaries, having nine friars, with 13 parish schools". Price, the Protestant bishop, reported that besides the Mass houses, there were eleven movable altars, thus making altogether 45 places where divine worship was celebrated. He stated further that the friaries were situate in Wexford and Ross, *the latter having been built within the last six years, and its large chapel within the last two years.* Both these friaries belonged to the Franciscans, the guardian of Wexford being Bonaventure Paye, and of Ross, Bonaventure Cormick, while the friary of Enniscorthy not included in the report had for guardian Columba Kavanagh (from Mr. J. W. Hanna's extracts.)

The date of Dr. Verdun's decease is readily determined by what Dr. Burke says of the translation of Dr. M'Egan from Clonmacnoise to Ferns. Stephen MacEgan, of the order of Friar Preachers, was consecrated bishop of Clonmacnoise on the 29th of Sept., 1725, by Pope Benedict XIII. In 1729 he received Apostolic letters transferring him to Ferns; but before the execution of the Papal decree he was appointed to Meath, vacant by the promotion of Dr. Luke Fagan to Dublin, Sept., 1729. Therefore Ferns became vacant before Meath, and the death of Dr. Verdun must have occurred some time before Sept., 1729, probably in the preceding year (*See Hib. Dom.*, p. 504).

F. AMBROSE CALLAGHAN, O.S.F., *suc.* 1729; *ob.* 1744.

In the year 1729, as has been just observed, the Right. Rev. Stephen M'Egan, Bishop of Clonmacnoise, a Dominican Friar, received a bull for his translation to Ferns, but he never took possession of the see. Before the execution of the Bull he was promoted to the nearer and more important see of Meath. (*Hib. Dom.*, p. 504). In consequence of this change, the Very Rev. F. Ambrose Callaghan, a native of Kildare, of the order of St. Francis, guardian formerly of St. Isidore's, Rome, and afterwards of the convent of Wexford in 1721, was appointed to the see of Ferns in 1729. He resided in his diocese, but assumed the name of *Dr. Walker*, in order to conceal himself and to save his life. There are some letters still extant in the Franciscan convent, Wexford, written in his firm legible hand, some signed *F. A. Callaghan*, and some *A. Walker*. I have now before me (Nov. 25, 1849), two beautiful specimens of his signature. Both these documents are signed by the bishop, but written by his secretary. By the first Dr. Sweetman is appointed treasurer, and by the second vicar-general, of the diocese of Ferns. Both documents are most creditable in matter and form, and show that in "the sorest times", to use their own burning words, the Irish prelates and priests were not unworthy of their high calling :

Ambrosius Dei et Apostolicae sedis gratia Epus. Ferns. dilecto in Christo filio Nicolao Sweetman salutem. Cum SSmus. Dominus noster Alexander Papa Septimus omnia beneficia infra Decanatum Revmis. Hiberniae Ordinariis, praesente Illmo. Domino Domino Gulielmo Archiepiscopo Cassiliensi conferenda indulserit, prout antecessori nostro Illmo. Domino Michaeli Rossiter, Episcopo Fernensi (sub cujus manu attestationem vidimus) retulit Illustrissimus Dominus Jacobus Epus. Ossoriens, cumque nunc temporis heterodoxi hujus dioecesis ordinarii, Catholicorum antiquam sequentes formam, quibus in foro externo succedere praesumunt, simili facultate gaudeant, quod nobis per diligentem inquisitionem certo constat. Nos talibus nixi fundamentis, ad bonum ecclesiae, dignitatem Thesaurarii nunc liberam et vacantem tibi praedicto Nicolao Sweetman, tanquam capaci et idoneo cum ejusdem juribus et pertinentibus conferimus.

Datum Wexfordiae sub manu et sigillo nostro die 26 Augusti, A.D. 1732.

De mandato Illutrisssimi Domini mei, Prosecretarius Nicolaus Sweetman.

AMBROSIUS EPISCOPUS FERNENSIS.

The penmanship throughout is excellent, but the bishop's name and title are written in a most beautiful hand. The other document signed by him, and dated Wexford, July 21, 1736, appoints Dr. Sweetman his vicar-general, and authorises him to make in his place the visitation of the diocese on this occasion, and to publish this letter of authorization in the several parishes. In neither of these orders, though formally signed and sealed, does he subscribe himself *Fr.* Ambrosius, etc., as was the custom of bishops promoted from religious orders. We give this important document in full, as it throws much light on Dr. Sweetman's life and character.

Ambrosius Dei et Apostolicae sedis gratia Epus. Fernensis, dilecto in Christo R. D. D. Nicolao Sweetman, S.T.D. Protonotario Apostolico, Ecclesiae Fernensis Thesaurario, necnon ecclesiae S. Fintani in Moyglasse rectori, etc., salutem in Domino. Cum rationabilibus de causis a munere vicariatus generalis in Dioecesi Fernensi eos non ita pridem amoverimus quibus ad illum exercendum facultates opportunas jam antea concesseramus; cumque similibus de causis consultum esse impraesentiarum ducamus, ut istiusmodi facultates et ipsum munus vicarii generalis iterum uni conferamus, et quidem uni potiusquam pluribus. Hinc te, quod a doctrina, bonis moribus, ac egregiis talentis sis toti dioecesi, sed et praecipue quod a zelo, sinceritate, candore, ac fidelitate, sis nobis enixius commendatus, et te unicum selegimus, quem nostrum in tota Dioecesi Fernensi vicarium generalem instituamus. Quapropter tenore ac vigore praesentium te nostrum vicarium generalem in tota Dioecesi Fernensi, ut praefertur, instituimus et declaramus, atque ita canonice institutum ac declaratum cum omnibus honoribus, praerogativis, et facultatibus in jure aut consuetudine vicariis hujusmodi concessis, universo hujus dioeceseos clero et populo commendamus, quatenus te veluti taliter institutum et declaratum venerentur ac recipiant, Tibi insuper communicamus facultates quas nostratibus Epis. dignata est concedere S. Sedes, ut autem notitia harum litterarum ad singulos quorum interest facilius perveniat, easdem inter visitandum (rogamus etenim ut dioecesim hac vice loco nostri visites) Parochis aliisque patefacias, et simul Apostolicis verbis eosdem exhorteris, ne desistant recordari vocationis suae et ut juxta Apostolicum monitum per bona opera certam eandem faciant, quo et mercedem a Christo pastore et medico animarum nostrarum recipiant et amplius in hac dioecesi quantumvis exulratis temporibus non vituperetur ministerium nostrucem. Datum Wexfordiae hac 21 Julii, A.D. 1736, sub nostro chirographo, et *dioecesis sigillo*, Ambros. Epus. Fernensis.

Dr. Callaghan died in 1744, and was buried in the chapel of Wexford.

NICHOLAS SWEETMAN, *suc.* 1744, *ob.* 1786.

Dr. Sweetman was born at Newbawn, county Wexford, of wealthy parents, and a highly respectable Catholic family. In the obituary notice in *Walker's Magazine*, it is stated that he was born in the county Kilkenny, of the family of Sweetmans of Castle Eve, near Callan ; but this is certainly a mistake. He made his college studies at St. Iago in Spain. We have noticed already how Dr. O'Callaghan appointed him treasurer of Ferns (August 26, 1732). The instrument conferring the canonry is in Dr. Sweetman's handwriting, signed by Ambrose Ferns, and sealed with the episcopal seal. On the 21st July, 1736, Dr. Sweetman was made Vicar-General, and in the parchment document, signed by Dr. Callaghan, and authenticated by a different episcopal seal, the new V.G. is styled :

" R. D. D. Nicolao Sweetman, S.T.D., Protonotario Apostolico, Ecclesiae Fernensis Thesaurario, necnon ecclesiae S. Fintani in Maglasse rectori, etc".

He was consecrated Bishop of Ferns in 1744.

At the very beginning of his administration he was engaged in more than one unpleasant controversy with the Franciscans in Wexford. The first arose immediately after his consecration, and regarded his right to rooms in the convent. Two of his predecessors resided there, but the Franciscans now disputed the right which he claimed to live in their house. As the question had been raised at all, they refused to admit the bishop even as a favour. Both parties appealed to Rome, and it was decided that the bishop had no right even by usage to rooms in the convent. The next dispute regarded the use of the convent church. There was then, as down to a recent period, but one chapel in the large town of Wexford, which was near, or rather immediately attached to, the convent. This chapel, the bishop contended, was the parochial one built by the people of the parish for their own use. The fathers maintained it was strictly conventual, and exclusively the property of their order. The Sunday collections were claimed by each party, although there was a secret understanding that when the fathers celebrated the offerings should be theirs. This dispute was also referred to the Holy See. The tradition of the Franciscans is that the Pope decided as before against the bishop, but that he, either anticipating or knowing the adverse sentence, proposed a compromise, which was accepted. By virtue of it, however suggested or brought about, the friars and the parochial clergy used afterwards the church in common. They received the collections in turn—every alternate Sunday and holiday, and both celebrated High Mass and gave holy Communion separately on Holy Thursday. This arrangement was carried out faithfully and with mutual forbearance down to our own time. But the memory of the struggle did not die out even with those who took the most active share in it.

I have before me records of the following appointments made by Dr. Sweetman, all given at Wexford, 1749 (50) :

February 16—The Rev. William Doyle to be P.P. of St. Laurence de Killurin cum annexis.

1767, April 2—Rev. Patrick Cullen, P.P. of Ballyellis cum annexis.

1773, March 20—Rev. Michael Fitzhenry, Prebend of Fethard.

1782, July 4—Rev. John Currin, P.P. Wexford, Treasurer.

1783, March 11—Rev. Patrick Doyle, Canon Lector.

Dr. Sweetman was a man of iron frame and great powers of body. It was said of him, that had he lived in the days of the Confederation, he would have been chosen unanimously general of the northern army. Perhaps it was this manly bearing that created the strongest suspicion when he was accused of treasonable practices. About the year 1752 an apostate priest gave information that the bishop was engaged in enlisting soldiers for the Pretender. On this silly charge he was arrested, and hurried away a prisoner to Dublin Castle to be tried for treason. But after a strict examination of himself and all his papers, which were also seized, it was found that there was not one particle of evidence against him, and he was honourably discharged from prison. The writer of the obituary in *Walker's Magazine*, Nov. 1786, thus notices Dr. Sweetman's arrest :

" He had been taken up and confined in the Castle of Dublin upon a malicious charge of high treason under the administration of the Duke of Dorset, in the year 1752, but the producing of all his papers and correspondence with the court of Rome proved highly honourable to himself and singularly advantageous to the Catholics of Ireland".

Nearly thirty years after, the same 'foul dishonouring' cry of treason was raised again, because Dr. Sweetman, when the whole county of Wexford rose in arms to assert their rights, gave some subscription to the volunteers.

"I have represented", writes Dr. Troy in reference to this charge, December 5, 1779, " your delicate situation to many who misinterpreted your subscription in favour of the Wexford Independent Volunteers, and made them sensible you could not act otherwise".

A Protestant dignitary went, perhaps, more directly to the principle which drew forth the subscription, when he described the Irish Catholics at that time as suffering " under a series of accumulated wrongs which would heighten the disgrace of human policy, if they could be paralleled in its annals".

Some of the secular clergy complained that Dr. Sweetman was too partial to his own relatives. I find no ground for the complaint, except that he promoted his nephew, Dr. Stafford, after a short service, to the parish of Rathangan, and afterwards, in 1773, recommended him as coadjutor, and that he gave the rich parish of Wexford to his grand-nephew, Dr. Currin. But the promotion of his relatives is no proof of nepotism, if the appointments were probably the best that could be made. Dr. Stafford won the respect and esteem of all who knew him, especially of Dr. Troy, no mean judge of character. He studied at St. Iago in Spain, was appointed P.P. of Rathangan in 1768, and coadjutor bishop (episcopus Dolichiensis *in partibus*) to his maternal uncle, Dr. Sweetman, in 1773. He made but one visitation of the diocese. On Sunday, September 30, 1781, when returning home after having baptized James Cardiff, afterwards surgeon to the 79th regiment, he was killed by a fall from his horse, and was buried in the Church of Tacumshane. On this sad occasion the following letter, condoling with Dr. Sweetman, was received from Dr. Troy :

MOST HONOURED AND REV. DEAR SIR,—A few weeks after my return to this place, I received the melancholy account of Dr. Stafford's death. I shall not at present renew your sorrow by expressing my own concern on the occasion, but do assure you nothing shall be wanting on my part to alleviate your affliction and conduce to your happiness. I understand Dr. Stafford's monthly remembrance is fixed for Tuesday instant; if it could be conveniently deferred till the Tuesday following, 6th November, I would make it a point to assist thereat and pay you my respects. Your answer will regulate my conduct in this particular. I shall therefore expect it, and am, with the greatest respect and esteem, Most Rev. dear sir, your most affectionate

J. T. TROY.

Kilkenny, October 16, 1781.   Dr. Sweetman, Wexford.

Dr. Currin governed the parish of Wexford with rare prudence and piety for about fifty years. It might be fairly contended, therefore, that Dr. Sweetman could not pass over the evident merits of these two relatives without injustice to themselves and great detriment to the Church. I believe Pius IV. did not escape the common charge of nepotism, when he appointed his young nephew, Charles Borromeo, Cardinal and Archbishop of Milan. Would that examples of such nepotism were frequent in the Church. I have several unpublished letters written to Dr. Sweetman, but very few of interest written by himself. Dr. Troy, both before and after his translation to Dublin, made it a rule to consult him on almost every question of importance. They differed often in their views—one siding with the people, and the other leaning to the Government. But their divergence in political opinions never interfered with their social intercourse. Their correspondence shows that they were bound by the ties of the closest friendship up to the very last day of Dr. Sweetman's life. Towards the close of 1772, Dr. Sweetman suffered a good deal from an ulcer in the leg, which made him unfit to perform the usual visitation of the diocese. The next year Dr. Stafford was appointed coadjutor bishop, and on his death Dr. James Caulfield was recommended by the bishop and chapter, and consecrated in 1782. Except the visitation, a very distressing work in those days, when every journey had to be made on horseback, Dr. Sweetman continued to discharge all his other episcopal duties zealously. They were not done merely in his name and by his authority: they were strictly his own personal acts. Even the official papers were written by himself. I have in my possession a document dated 11th March, 1783, appointing Patrick Doyle, Canon Lectoral of the Cathedral of Ferns, and the handwriting is as firm and legible as it was fifty years before, when Dr. Sweetman himself was first appointed a member of the same chapter. Yet his health was failing fast for years before. In the beginning of 1778 his life was despaired of for some days from what his medical advisers pronounced to be apoplexy. On his partial recovery from this attack, Dr. Troy wrote the following letter :

MOST HON. AND DEAR SIR,—Mr. Colfer showed me your last favour to him, giving an account of your recovery from the fit you mentioned, which I hope was not of an apoplectic kind. Whether or not, your friends rejoiced at your escape, and I in particular wish you a long enjoyment of the *mens hilaris in corpore sano*. The form of excommunication used by me in regard to the unhappy Bonny Cummins, may be seen in the Roman Pontifical towards the end. I explained the nature of it from different altars, after describing the scandalous life of the incorrigible culprit. I returned hither from Dublin on the 3rd instant, and I have been since employed in visiting some neighbouring parishes. I shall, please God, be at Thomastown next Monday, and at Inisteague the Wednesday following. I would be very glad to see Mr. Caulfield of Ross at either place. Dr. Carpenter informed you of his sentiments relative to the test-oath. As they coincide with mine, I shall for the present refer you to his letters on this subject, but shall explain myself fully to Mr. Caulfield. The alarmed Protestant's strictures on my pastoral letter, and the different replies, etc., have been unaccountably mislaid. I cannot, therefore, comply with my sincere promise of sending them to you. Your seraphic countryman here pays his respects to you; mine to Dr. Stafford: and be persuaded I am, with great respect and esteem, most hon. dear Sir,

Your assured friend and very humble servant,

J. T. TROY.

Kilkenny, 24th September, 1778.   Dr. Sweetman, Wexford.

December 23, same year, Dr. Troy wrote again thus:

MOST REV. AND DEAR SIR,—As neither turn-coats, turn-coat makers, or any other denomination of miscreants, can cause an alteration in my sincere regard and esteem for you; I sit down to wish you from my heart many happy returns of the approaching holy season, with every desirable blessing, and heaven in reversion. It gives me pleasure to find by your last agreeable favour of the 4th ultimo, that you regard our difference of opinion relative to the test in a political sense, without suspecting my orthodoxy. As I have long reconciled my mind to the formulary, I think I cannot but follow the example of our confreres, who already have sworn, or are resolved to appear in order to subscribe it. My affection for you shall remain inviolate, although our speculations on that subject are opposite. I have declared my opinion and resolution to my clergy, without an injunction on any person to adopt them. I wish you long life, without the mortification of burying your younger friends, and am most sincerely and respectfully, with compliments to Dr Stafford, most hon. dear friend,

Your affectionate and very humble servant,

J. T.

Kilkenny, 23rd December, 1778.   Dr. Sweetman, Wexford.

With this highly characteristic and friendly address we must close our extracts from the Troy correspondence.

Dr. Sweetman's death is thus recorded in *Walker's Hibernian Magazine* for November, 1786: "Died in Wexford, aged 90, the Right Rev. Nicholas Sweetman, titular Lord Bishop of Ferns, which bishopric he had enjoyed for 42 years".

Dr. Sweetman died on the 19th of October, 1786, and was buried in the Church of Clougeen.

JAMES CAULFIELD, *cons.* 1782; *ob.* .

Dr. Caulfield was born in the year 1732 in the county Wexford, and was ordained priest by Dr. Sweetman in 1757, before beginning his ecclesiastical studies, as was the custom in those days. He studied for eight years in the College of St. Thomas at Seville under the Dominicans, where he took out his degree of Doctor of Divinity. After his return to Ireland he served first as curate, then as parish priest of New Ross in 1771, and in the year following was made Vicar-General of his native diocese. Upon the death of Dr. Stafford in 1781, he was postulated for by Dr. Sweetman, and appointed coadjutor bishop, with the title of *Epus. Birthensis in partibus*, Feb. 26, 1782, and consecrated July 7, 1782, by Dr. Carpenter of Dublin, assisted by Dr. Troy and (by Apostolic Indult) the Very Rev. Bernard Downes, Dean of Ferns. For these facts, we have, besides other proof, Dr. Caulfield's own testimony. The following is a copy of the highly flattering testimonial which the superiors of Seville sent at his request to the Papal Nuncio at Brussels on November 1, 1763:

Excellentissime Domine, cum D. Jacobus Caulfield, ex Hibernia ortus, Dioecesis Fernensis alumnus, presbyter secundum S.R. Ecclesiae ritum titulo missionis Hiberniae ordinatus, defectu studiorum ex sua patria coactus fuerit, hucque ad illa prosequenda, quo dictae missioni magis idoneus aptusque reddatur pervenerit; atque nobiscum de quodam onere a suo ordinario sibi inter recipiendum ordines, tactis evangeliis imposito communicaret, viz. ut e sua patria ad dictum studiorum finem egressus, non prius reversurus quam diploma litterasve patentes Excellentissimi Domini Bruxellensis nuntii habuisset; cumque nunc peractis studiis, de regressu in suam patriam cogitans, nos solicite humiliter tamen rogavit ut illum ad praefatum diploma impetrandum adjuvaremus. Nos igitur infra scripti Rector regens ac collegiales cathedratici, S. Theologiae et artium almi majoris collegii ac generales studiorum scholae publicae Pontificiae ac caesareae ac regiae Divi Thomae Aquinatis ordinis Praedicatorum, civitatis Hispalensis, attendentes petitionibus, etc., et annuere volentes asserimus, harumque tenore fidem facimus, et declaramus dictum D. Jac. Caulfield in publicis scholis nostris Philosophiae cathedras tribus integris annis, sacraeque Theologiae totidem attente, solicite, sineque notabili interruptione audivisse, actibusque interioribus exterioribusque astitisse, vel conclusiones defensando, vel argumenta subtiliter proponendo, quae omnia singulaque viri scholastici munia ingenti omnium plausu, propria utilitate ac grandi proventu fuisse exercitum. Quibus omnibus recognitis ac rite consideratis praedictum Jacobum dignum aptumque, qui missionarii munus suscipiat, ejusque fungatur officiis censemus et judicamus: exinde vestram Excellentiam supplicamus impensiusque rogamus, ut illi dictum diploma vel literas concedere et huc remittere dignetur, quo Omnipotentem orabit nobiscum vestram Excellentiam multos annos incolumem servare.

Hispali 1° Nov. A D. 1763. Ad Excell. Dominum suae sanctitatis Nuncium, Bruxellis.

When appointed coadjutor he obtained from Rome leave to retain his parish of New Ross:

Ex audientia SSmi. habita die 23 Junii, 1782. Relatis per me infra scriptum S. Cong. de Propag. Fide secretm. precibus R. R. D. Jacobi Caulfield Epi. Birthensis, coadjutoris Ecclesiae Fernensis in Hibernia, qui humillime supplicavit pro *retentione* parochiae de Ross sive Rospontis in eadem dioecesi, ut nimirum ex illius fructibus congruam sustentationem, quam aliunde non habet percipiat. SSmus. D.D. Pius VI., benigne indulsit ut praefatus coadjutor in commendam et pro mensali juxta loci consuetudinem eandem parochiam Rospontinam retinere et tanquam parochus administrare valeat, donec aliter per S. sedem provideatur, quibuscumque in contrarium non obstantibus.

Datum Romae ex aedibus S. Cong. die et anno quibus supra.

On the third page of the preceding " ex audientia" sheet is a letter to Dr. Caulfield, dated Rome, 28th August, 1782 (marked " received September 20, answered November 26, 1782") from Charles Kelly, the famous Dominican of the Minerva, dean of the Roman Cassanate, and agent for many years of Dr. Troy and his friends. He was descended of a highly distinguished family in the county Roscommon, and heir to his father's large estate, which he gave up to a younger brother, whose daughter married The O'Connor, the lineal descendant of the last Irish monarch. Father Charles Kelly died in the Dominican Convent at Rome in 1793. His name occurs often in the Irish correspondence with Rome, from the year 1770 until his death. The letter begins thus:

"MOST REV. SIR,—I had the pleasure and satisfaction of reading your edifying letter of the 3rd of June. I knew not where you had studied, nor those particulars which attached you with some distinction to the holy order I unworthily profess [allusion to the fact that Dr. C. studied under the Dominican Professors at Seville]. Now I clearly see how strongly cemented is, and should be, the friendship subsisting between Dr. Troy and you, which, as extended on your side to the whole body, justly claims our acknowledgments. If ever, you may believe, I most cordially congratulate you on the function [Dr. C.'s consecration] of 7th July last, and I pray God to alleviate by His grace that burden of which you feel the weight. . . . . I delivered to Cardinal Antonelli the letter for him enclosed in yours to me of the 15th of July. He read it in my presence with great satisfaction. He is puzzled now to get such another as you for the coadjutorship of Kildare. I could suggest none, but told him the prelates of that province would, I was sure, soon recommend a subject of their own way of thinking, which indeed is desirable, if not necessary, in the present circumstances. We are here impatient to know what has been resolved in the assembly of the prelates of Armagh and Cashel. The protest of the northern districts of the former against Dr. Reilly has not as yet appeared here. Is it probable they waited for the opinion of the prelates assembled?"

He concludes by saying there is no need of sending the oath of consecration to Rome, and that Dr. Troy thinks Dr. C. should apply for another parish *in commendam,* as being necessary for his proper maintenance during the lifetime of the old bishop. He succeeded to the see of Ferns in 1786, not in 1785, as in the Roman Notizie " fatto Vescovo nel 1785".

I have before me (March 14, 1850), the relatio Ecclesiae which he prepared to send to Rome in 1796, the tenth year after he became Bishop of Ferns. From this I quote the following :

"Jacobus Caulfield, dioecesis Fernensis oriundus, sacerdos saecularis ordinatus anno 1757 ab illustrissimo ac Reverendissimo Nicolao Sweetman ad titulum Missionis Hibernicae, studiorum causa in *Hispaniam* profectus, et iisdem per octennium in collegio majore D. Thomae Aquinatis Hispalensi incumbens, et Doctoratus in S. Theologiae gradu insignitus".

After stating the reason (ill-health) for leaving college sooner than he intended, Dr. Caulfield adds :

" Sui ordinarii jussu vicario generali Fernensi in Parochia rurali deserviens per quadriennium, tandem anno 1771 parochus et Rector S. Mariae Rosspontensis (seu de Ross) et initio anni sequentis Thesaurarius Fernensis et vicarius generalis episcopi constitutus fuit. Anno 1781 Illustrissimo ac Revmo. Joanne Stafford, episcopi Dolichiensi in partibus in meliorem vitam vocato, postulantibus et supplicantibus Nicolao Epo. et capitulo

Fernensi, commendantibus quoque Provinciae Dub praesulibus, Episcopus Birthensis in partibus et coadjutor Fernensis nominatus et constitutus fuit, die 26 Feb. an. 1782, consecrationis vero beneficium septimo Julii, 1782, ab archiepiscopo Dubliniensi accepit, assistentibus, Joanne Thomae Troy, tunc Ossoriensi nunc vero Dublin., et ex indulto Apostolico amplissimo D. Bernardo Downes, Decano Fernensi".

Dr. Caulfield continued to assist the aged bishop, and to give him a full report each month of all the changes in the diocese, until Dr. Sweetman's death, 19th October, 1786, as in the relatio :

" Usque ad diem 19 Octob. an. 1786, quam Deo vocante clausit ultimum".

In the same report I find an interesting account of the general state of the diocese. Ferns is described as thirty-eight miles long and twenty broad, with eight borough towns, which return each two members to Parliament, viz. Wexford, Ross, Enniscorthy, and the towns of Taghmon, Feathard, Clomines, Bannow, and Gorey. The diocese has a chapter of nineteen members, viz. five dignitaries, Dean, Precentor, Chancellor, Treasurer, and Archdeacon ; four canons—*de officio* (*ut vocantur*), nempe Doctoralis, Theologalis, Lectoralis, et Poenitentiarius, and ten Prebendaries—Kilbrane, Fethard, Edermine, Taghmon, Kilrush, Toombe, Clone, Whitechurch, Crosspatrick, and Colstioff. It had 143 parishes, but now only thirty-six parish priests, and some of them without curates. It had seventeen monasteries of canons regular of S. Austin ; three Priories of Templars, afterwards Knights of St. John of Jerusalem ; one Benedictine Priory at Glascarrig ; and two Cistercian abbeys—Dunbrody and Tintern ; three Reformed

Franciscan Convents—Wexford, Ross, Enniscorthy; two of Hermits of St. Austin—Ross and Clomine, and one of Carmelites. It never had any nunnery.

There are now only four *hospitia* or houses of Regulars, a Franciscan Convent at Wexford, with six friars leading a community life, and using a public church, which is also parochial; one of Hermits of St. Austin at Ross, with a public chapel of their own, the number of Friars being two or three; another of hermits near Clonmine, with only one Friar; and one of Carmelites at Little Hanton, with only one Friar; neither of these two last has a chapel. In the *relatio* it is added that Dr. Caulfield has never been absent a week from the diocese, except once for two months at the Lucan Spa, and then with the knowledge and approval of Archbishop Troy. He has not ventured to call a Diocesan Synod for fear of gentry and Protestants, nor has there been any Provincial Synod since his appointment. He obtained permission by letters of August 2, 1795, to use the fines for dispensations in banns and in the forbidden degrees. He has no good work to boast of, but giving vestments and ornaments to the chapel of New Ross, and helping to build and furnish other chapels. His means are limited, hardly adequate for his support and the livery of two horses for himself and servant. His parish priests keep registers of baptisms and marriages, but not of the number confirmed or of deaths. Of a total population amounting to 120,000, there are at least 114,000 Catholics, and only eighty priests, including Regulars. Hence confessors must often spend eight, ten, or twelve hours a day in the confessional.

Conferences in cases of conscience and sacred rites are held in Ferns from April to November, attended by all the seculars, generally by the Friars, and often presided over by the bishop.

The people are not improving in piety or in obedience to their spiritual or temporal rulers—nay, they are becoming more licentious and disorderly. The " White Boys", who formed their illegal society in Munster a few years ago, spreading thence to the diocese of Ossory, threatened Ferns too. They owed their success to the secret and cunning intrigues of Protestants, who urged them to rise up against the oppressive tithes and exactions of the parsons. They were succeeded by the " Right Boys", who bound themselves by secret oaths, and forbade not only the payment of tithes, but also the usual offerings to their own clergy. Dr. Caulfield, alarmed at this irreligious spirit, after consulting with the Bishop of Ossory, denounced the leaders and threatened censures. But to no purpose. In his own diocese three or four parishes rose up *en masse*, bound by oath to attain these objects, swearing others at the chapel gates, and threatening death to every one who declined to perjure himself. At last a large multitude proceeded to Wexford to liberate two prisoners of their society, and resolved to burn the town in case their demand was not granted. A strong company of soldiers met them as they entered the town. A desperate engagement ensued. Many of the unhappy people were killed or severely wounded. On the side of the military not one was killed but the officer in command, who fell in the very beginning of the action. The untrained crowd was completely routed, and the defeat taught them to be more docile and attentive to the counsels of their best friends. The report concludes thus:

"Huc usque scripseram usque ad diem Februarii 3tium anno 1796".

The good bishop little thought of the worse evils that soon befell his people : he had no idea then of the savage slaughter that ensued shortly after. That he strove manfully and zealously to put down every seditious movement is manifest from the history of his whole life. Yet, as it seems to have been the hereditary privilege of the bishops of Ferns to be charged with compassing treason, Dr. Caulfield could not hope to escape at a very critical period, when almost the whole county, of which he had the spiritual care, rose in open rebellion. A false and malignant and scurrilous attack was made on him and his clergy by Sir Richard Musgrave in his *Memoirs of the Different Rebellions in Ireland, with a particular detail of that which broke out on the 23rd of May*, 1798. Dr. Caulfield was accused, 1) of neglect in reporting to the Government the preparations of the United Irishmen ; 2) of indifference in rendering aid to loyal Protestants ; 3) of open treason in encouraging the rebels and blessing the pikemen in the streets of Wexford. In a pamphlet, which went through several editions, entitled "*The Reply of the Right Rev. Dr. Caulfield*, Roman Catholic Bishop of Wexford, and of the Roman Catholic clergy of Wexford, to the misrepresentations of Sir Richard Musgrave, Bart., these charges are ably refuted. The bishop answers, 1) That he knew no more than what every man of common observation was perfectly aware of, namely, that the people were for more than four years irritated, disconted, and inattentive to the warning of their own clergy, and he calls God to witness that the first idea he had of the rebellion was from the Government proclamations; 2) Whenever he and his clergy could save life or property, they used all their influence for that purpose; but their authority and warnings were not heeded by the misguided victims of irreligious leaders; 3) he never blessed any body of insurgents, and could not have done so at the time and place alleged, because he never left his house that day. This statement, sworn to in the most solemn manner by Dr. Caulfield, supported by depositions on oath of several clergymen and laymen of respectability, and confirmed by the express and grateful acknowledgments of the highest civil and military authorities, did not satisfy the titled assailant, who repeated all his calumnies in a more offensive form in "*Observations* on the reply of Right Rev. Dr. Caulfield", published in Dublin 1802. He speaks of the Catholic bishop as a man "that has no regard whatever to truth", and the priests "as anointed impostors" "guilty of flagrant impudence", "notorious falsehoods", etc. With such an adversary, Dr. Caulfield prudently declined to contend any further. His cause was espoused by Vindex in a temperate and able pamphlet, and by Plowden, a more skilled hand in polemical strife.

Just as Plowden's 'Reply' was about to issue from the press, he and his publisher were threatened by the worthy baronet, who was unscrupulous in assailing others, with an action for libel, and the 'Reply' had to be modified and partly withdrawn through fear of oppressive law proceedings. Referring to this subject, Dr. Troy wrote thus to a lay friend, August 15, 1803 :

MY DEAR SIR,—One of Sir Richard Musgrave's worst calumnies is his assertion that none of our prelates, except Dr. Moylan, enforced the duty of loyalty when the rebellion of 1798 commenced. I expected that Mr. Plowden would have proved the contrary by a reference to the *Collection of Remonstrances* published by Coghlan. I also hoped that Dr. Bellew would have been vindicated by the insertion of Mr. Cooke's short letter to him, and the affidavits I enclosed to you for Mr. Plowden, who completely vindicates Dr. Caulfield, Bishop of Ferns. It is to be regretted that Mr. Plowden could not publish the mentioned and other documents. I frequently desired Messrs. Keating to send me half a dozen copies of the *Remonstrances*, etc., and beg they may be forwarded to me without delay. I intend to have them republished here, with additional ones. I have not a single copy of them. One priest only has been apprehended since the late insurrection. He is parish priest in the diocese of Ross and county Cork, and was discharged in less than twenty-four hours. Nevertheless, some of the English papers state that priests sitting in committee have been taken up. *Falkner's Journal* stated that Connolly of *Maynooth College* was in Kilmainham Jail. A schoolmaster of that name, who taught in the village, but in no manner connected with the college, is the person in prison See President Dunn's declaration on that subject, published in all our newspapers of Tuesday last. I have been honoured with several letters from England, complimenting me on the late printed exhortation occasioned by that wicked insurrection here on the 23rd ultimo. Amongst others, from Lords Cornwallis, Hertford, Castlereagh, Sir J. C. Hippisley, and Mr. Corry. We are apparently quiet here. We were so on Friday, the 22nd ultimo. French intrigue and gold will, I fear, fan the flame of rebellion, which seems extinguished. May God protect us, and direct our poor, over credulous people. All friends are well.

Believe me, my dear sir, faithfully yours,

Dublin, 15th August, 1803. ✠ J. T. TROY.

In 1803 Dr. Caulfield's health failed so much that he found it necessary to apply for a coadjutor. Though his name appears in some of the public documents after that date, he took no distinguished part in the many important political and religious questions that caused such a ferment in this country during the imprisonment and exile of Pius VII. He signed the ill-advised resolutions of January, 1799, sanctioning the principle of the veto and provision for the clergy " under certain regulations not incompatible with their doctrine and discipline"; but he and the other prelates who were present at that meeting, voted also unanimously for the famous resolution adopted at their assembly in Dublin on the 14th September, 1808, condemning the veto, and for the address against both the veto and the pensioning of the clergy, unanimously adopted at the meetings held also in Dublin, February 24, 1810. On this last occasion alone is Dr. Caulfield represented as voting by proxy. Yet it is unlikely that in his old age and very delicate health he was able to travel to Dublin in 1810, or even in 1808. His name was signed to the appeal, December 1, 1809, of Drs. Troy, Bray, and six other bishops, to the prelates of the western province to retract their proceedings against the Rev. Oliver Kelly, Vicar-Capitular of Tuam, canonically elected; " but it was well known that he was not at the meeting alluded to, nor at all in Dublin *for years past*, owing to his advanced age and concomitant infirmities". (Report of the proceedings of the Connaught bishops, p. 18). Dr. Caulfield died January 14, 1814, and was buried in the chapel of Wexford.

PATRICK RYAN, *consec.* 1805; *ob.* 1819.

Through the very great kindness of the nearest surviving relative of Dr. Ryan, we are enabled to give the following account of his family. About the year 1700 Edward Ryan, the bishop's great-grandfather, descended of an ancient Irish stock, removed from the old family residence at Ballycarran to a house lately built in an adjoining part of the estate called Ballinakill, within a few miles of Kilcock, in the county Kildare, where he died soon after. He was succeeded by his son Thomas, who died at an early age, leaving issue two sons, James and Edward, and three daughters. 1. James married Bridget Barnwall, daughter of Robert Barnwall, Esq., county Meath, and resided at Newcastle, county Meath, after his marriage.

2. Edward Ryan succeeded his father in Ballinakill, and married the daughter of Philip O'Reilly, Esq., of Coolamber and Ballymorris, county Longford. They were blessed with a numerous offspring, two daughters and eleven sons. Thomas, the eldest son, who inherited the estate, married, April 19, 1798, Mary, eldest daughter of Edward and Magdalen Byrne, of Byrne's Hill, county Dublin. Philip, the second of the eleven brothers, went to Copenhagen, and there married (first) a Danish lady, the daughter of Baron Firsh, and after her death married (secondly) a Miss Farrell, born in Denmark, but, as the name implies, of Irish extraction.

Patrick, the third of the brothers, the future bishop, was born in 1768 at the family mansion at Ballinakill, where his father, Edward Ryan, died in his 55th year, of fever. The bishop's mother lived to a great old age, and died at Blackhall, county Meath, in her son Edward's house, December 17, 1828.

We should not dwell on these details only that it has been often and confidently asserted that Dr. Ryan was a native of the diocese of Ferns, and the assertion has been repeated and sanctioned by a recent clever and popular writer, who says further that the bishop was brother of a banker. This statement is inaccurate in both its parts. Every one of the eleven brothers was born in the same house at Ballinakill, county Kildare, and though, like many other educated Catholic youths, who saw no chance of promotion at home, three or four of the Ryans were forced to seek honourable service in strange lands; not one of them ever held a share in a bank. John, the fourth brother, joined the Spanish army; Bernard, the fifth, entered the East India Company's service; James, the sixth, the well-known correspondent, J. R., of Charles James Fox, was an extensive wine merchant in Dublin, partner in the firm of Byrne, McDonnell, and Co., then the first commercial house in the city; Edward, the seventh, lived at Newcastle first, and then at Blackhall, county Meath; George, the eighth, died in Copenhagen, December 6, 1861, the last survivor of the brothers; William and Richard died young; and Joseph, the youngest brother, a gentleman of refined taste, kind and hospitable, after spending many years at Barcelona in Spain, came to reside at the Grove, county Meath.

To return to the bishop's personal history. From his childhood, Patrick Ryan showed a decided leaning for the ecclesiastical state, and was sent, therefore, with the full approval of his pious parents, to Rome to pursue his studies. He must have entered college before 1788, as I find among Dr. Troy's letters one of that date to him, enclosing money from his father. At the end of the usual course he was ordained priest, and returned to Dublin in the spring of 1793. His first mission was in the parish of St. Nicholas, and while still a curate there, he was admitted to the chapter as Prebendary of Wicklow, his successor being Daniel Murray. On the 5th January, 1803, he was appointed Secretary to the Board of Trustees, Maynooth College, and on the 2nd of October, 1804 (date of Bull), coadjutor bishop of Ferns, with title of *Germanicia in partibus*. February 15, 1805, he wrote from Dublin to several bishops, announcing his appointment as coadjutor, and stating that he had received from Mr. Marsden, on the part of the government, promise of support and protection in the discharge of his episcopal functions in Wexford. He could not, however, leave Dublin until April, and would gladly retain his office of secretary to the Maynooth Board with even the small salary of £56 19s. 6d., no provision being yet made for him in Wexford. In these letters he recommended a Mr. Barrett of Carlow for the rhetoric chair in Maynooth. The college trustees, with that paternal regard for personal feeling and interest which has ever been characteristic of their rule, allowed Dr. Ryan to keep his office until he resigned of his own accord on July 7th, 1807.

After his consecration in 1805, Dr. Ryan assisted most punctually at the councils of the Irish bishops, and acted very often as their secretary. Thus we find him at the meetings of 14th September, 1808, against the veto ; of 24th and 26th February, 1810, when the resolution of 1808 was solemnly renewed in a public address to the clergy and laity; and of 18th November, 1812, condemning Blanchard and Columbanus. He also signed the pastoral address of the bishops, May 26, 1813, against the *securities* in the relief bill, and the congratulatory letter to Pius VII., ordered at Maynooth May 27th, 1814. In this last document for the first time he assumed the title of Bishop of Ferns, his illustrious predecessor having died in the beginning of the same year.

Long before the death of Dr. Caulfield, the government of the diocese was in reality left to Dr. Ryan, who was young and vigorous, and well able to bear hard work. Besides the usual cares of his sacred office, he had to face, from the very beginning, dangers which in Ireland happily are not often to be met with. It was against these that he had the promise of *protection* from the government. For a long time after the rebellion, the priests of Wexford were kept in terror of their lives by a bigoted faction, who went about in the open day prepared with instruments of death. Priests were insulted in the public highways, and sometimes interfered with in their most sacred duty, as in their visits to the sick and dying. Dr. Ryan resolved at any risk to put down this intolerant spirit, and took what may be considered a strange way of effecting his purpose. The Orangemen were gathered together in large numbers in Enniscorthy on one of their great anniversaries, when, to their utter surprise, the bishop, accompanied by one lay gentleman of influence, entered the meeting. Having asked permission to say a few words to the gentlemen present on a subject of great interest to himself and the Catholics of Wexford, he appealed to them in a calm and most solemn manner not to goad their brethren into resistance by offensive words and displays. He assured them the Catholics were ready to forget all past wrongs and differences, and to live at peace with their fellow-countrymen. For his own part, his most sacred duty was to preach and practise Christian charity, and he would never yield to fear or force in the discharge of his ministry. The short speech was well received, and produced the best effect. From that day party demonstration ceased in a great measure, and there was no further interference with the free exercise of religion. But although this danger passed away, the bishop's health was much impaired by the struggle and strife, and by constant anxiety and labour. There was hardly a day that he did not spend eight or nine hours in the confessional. He preached morning and evening on Sundays, and visited nearly every parish in the diocese each year. Under this heavy strain his bodily strength failed, and a sudden and violent attack of paralysis weakened even his mental faculties. He died at Enniscorthy on the 9th March, 1819.

A mural slab of white marble in the Church of Enniscorthy, where his remains are laid, is thus inscribed :

Illustriss. et Reverendiss.
Patricius Ryan, Eps. Fernensis, natus
A.D. 1768.
Expleto studiorum ecclesiasticorum curriculo
ad animarum curam vocatus, et ab Archiepo.
Dubliniensi parochiae Clontarf pastor est
institutus A.D. 1797.
Coadjutor Epi. Fern. creatus A.D. 1805,
ipso jam defuncto in ministerium Episcopale

pleno jure successit A.D. 1814. Primus sedem Ep. in civitate Enniscorthiensi collocavit, et disciplinae Ecclesiasticae excolendae atque saluti animarum promovendae per annos quatuordecim sedulo intentus, supremum diem obiit VII. Idus Martii, 1819.
R. I. P.

JAMES KEATING, *suc.* 1819 ; *ob.* 1849.

James Keating was born in the year 1783, of Michael Keating and Margaret Cummins. His father rented an extensive farm, which his second son, Michael, still held in 1851, near the town of Enniscorthy, whither the bishop's grand-father emigrated from the Barony of Forth, the ancestral home. The bishop's father was a pious, practical Catholic, and a true patriot when love of country demanded many a painful sacrifice.

James, the subject of our memoir, learned classics in Wexford. He was grown up a young man in appearance, if not in years, in the famous year of the rebellion, and witnessed many of its sanguinary excesses. On one occasion during the reign of terror he had a narrow escape of his life On Whit Sunday in 1798, when standing a little outside the house of a friend, with whom he lodged while at school, about midway from Wexford to Enniscorthy, he was deliberately fired at by some straggling yeomen. As soon as he perceived the danger, he leaped from the road fence into a willow plantation, and in the fall dislocated his toe, which was never after restored to its socket. Through life he referred reluctantly, and not without deep feeling, to what he himself had seen during the insurrection; but whenever in social intercourse he did allude to what was manifestly a painful topic, his conversation became entertaining and animated, and his memory of preceding times seemed to be vivid and distinct. Dr. Keating entered Maynooth College for logic, September 29, 1804, received clerical tonsure on Friday, June 7, 1805, minor orders in 1806, subdeaconship in 1807, deaconship on Saturday, June 11, 1808, and was ordained priest in the summer of the same year. In the early part of his college course he stood *in prima classe*, yet obtained no prize until his second year's divinity, when he got second premium in dogmatic theology. During the summer vacation of 1808, Archbishop Troy wrote to Dr. Caulfield an urgent letter, requesting his Lordship to allow some of the young priests of Ferns to serve for a time on the mission of Dublin, where the harvest was great and the labourers few. Dr. Caulfield, anxious to comply with his Grace's request, ordained Mr. Keating, and then announced to him his wish that he should devote himself for a time to the ministry in Dublin. The young priest was too modest and humble not to assent to the least intimation of his superior's will as a call from heaven. He obeyed at once unhesitatingly, and applied to the coadjutor bishop, Dr. Ryan, for letters of introduction to Dr. Troy. Bishop Ryan advised him to defer his journey to Dublin for a few days, adding that he himself would explain to Dr. Caulfield the pressing wants of his own diocese. At that very time the services of another priest were much needed in the *mensal* parish of Camolin, and Mr. Keating was first appointed curate of that parish, then administrator, and continued in that office until his appointment as coadjutor to Dr. Ryan. Before the concordat of 1829, the manner of postulation for Irish bishops varied very much in different dioceses. In Ferns the usage was to assemble *all the clergy*, who recommended three priests to the Holy See. When Dr. Ryan applied for a coadjutor, Mr. Keating's name was only second on the list of those recommended by the priests. He had, therefore, little appehension that he should be chosen before one for whom he voted himself, and regarded as eminently fit for the episcopal dignity. He was accordingly much surprised when, on his way to a station in the remotest part of the parish, he received a letter from Dr. Troy, announcing his appointment. At first he could not bring himself to believe that the letter was genuine, and proceeded with anxious mind to his labour of charity. When his work was over, he rode home quickly, and showed the letter to his brother priests, who zealously but vainly solicited him not to resist the will of God. Next day he started for Dublin, visited Dr. Troy (by whom he was warmly congratulated), and expressed his firm resolution to decline the proffered dignity. Dr. Troy reasoned with him calmly, pointed out the inconvenience of delay and the inutility of seeking to be relieved from the burden, and finally exhorted him to trust in the Divine protection. Dr. Keating listened respectfully, but in the end declared that his resolution could not be shaken. He never could undertake such an office. " Well, then, young friend", rejoined Dr. Troy playfully, " you have shoulders to bear a heavier weight", alluding to Dr. Keating's almost gigantic stature ; " if you will have your own way, send a formal resignation to the Cardinal Prefect. You must, however, keep the Brief until he allows you to return it: and remember", he added emphatically, in a kind but firm tone, "I shall also write to his Eminence by the same post, and implore of him not to heed your apology; and I think, sir, I have more influence in Rome than you. I tell you, then once for all, your exertions will be bootless; spare yourself and me the trouble of this correspondence". He was at length forced to yield, and remained for a few days in Dublin, making some arrangements for his consecration. In the meantime, Dr. Ryan died unexpectedly, and was buried before Dr. Keating's return to Enniscorthy.

A very unusual difficulty arose about the consecration. Dr. Keating was appointed Bishop of *Antinoe in partibus*, and coadjutor to the Bishop of Ferns, with right of succession. The document from Rome was formal in every respect, dated January 12, 1819; but by a strange blunder on the part of the Roman copyist, he was described in the beginning of the brief as coadjutor to Patrick, Bishop of Ferns, and in the end, where the right of succession is conferred, as coadjutor to George, Bishop of Elphin. The mistake arose from the fact that the same clerk was engaged in transcribing both Briefs—one for Ferns, the other for Elphin—at the same time. In consequence of this error, Dr. Keating was consecrated not as Bishop of Ferns, but simply as Bishop of Antinoe, on the 21st March, 1819. He governed the diocese as *Vicar-Capitular* until a new Brief reached him, removing all doubt as to right of succession. Most of these particulars regarding Dr. Keating's life after leaving college, I had from his own lips on the 17th August, 1849, just three weeks before his death. He was then in vigorous health, though suffering slightly from gout. Few who saw him at that time could suppose that the final issue was so near as it proved to be. But we know not the day nor the hour.

As a bishop, he was active and zealous, and deserving all the high praise bestowed on him in the obituary notice in *The Tablet* of September 15, 1849. In politics he faithfully followed the guidance of O'Connell, differing from him only on the poor laws, and even then not openly. He was an earnest Antivetoist, joined heartily in the struggles for Emancipation and Repeal of the Union, and against the Tithes, the Bequests Bill, Mixed Education, the 'godless' colleges, and deplored to the last the ill-advised secession of the Young Ireland Party. As a preacher he was effective, sometimes reaching a high order of eloquence. His massive figure and noble bearing attracted attention even when his words failed to produce effect. The splendid monuments raised by him in the town of Enniscorthy are abiding proofs of his zeal. There he built, from a design by A. W. Pugin, a fine Gothic Church, the first of that style in our times in the United Kingdom. He provided two large schools for the poor children, and built a beautiful convent for the Presentation nuns. In these and like works of charity his whole time and resources were expended. The injury which he received in youth already referred to, prevented his taking much exercise on foot, and brought on at last sharp attacks of gout. But his vigorous frame seemed to be proof against this slow disease. For the last nine months of his life he suffered a good deal from a tumor under the right ear, which, though it gradually wasted his strength, caused for a long time no serious alarm. It turned out, however, to be incurable cancer, from the effects of which he died at 8 p.m. on Friday, the 7th September, 1849, leaving behind him few more sincere friends or more zealous and learned priests. His remains were solemnly interred the following Tuesday, September 11th, in the new Church of Enniscorthy, the noblest material memorial of his piety and munificence. There is no monument or inscription over the grave, but on a mural slab is inscribed the following epitaph :

Illustriss. et Reverendiss. Jacobus Keating, Epus.
Fernensis, e diœcesi Fernensi oriundus, natus est
A.D. 1783.
In collegio Manutiano S. Patritii, studiis
ecclesiasticis summa cum laude expletis,
ordinem presbyteratus suscepit 1809.
In vinea Domini operarius fidelis et impiger,
Ecclesiae Fernensi regendae Epus. praeficitur,
XII Kalend. April, A.D. 1819.
Munus Episcopale per triginta annos, prudentia
animi, virtute et moderatione, necnon pietate
erga Deum et homines spectabilis exercuit.
Libertatem Ecclesiae acerrime vindicavit, et demum
hac cathedrali summo cum studio divini
honoris labores inter plurimos et graves
temporum angustias extructa,
animam placide Deo reddidit
VII Idus Sept. A.D. 1849.
R. I. P.

INSCRIPTION UNDER MEMORIAL WINDOW OF STAINED GLASS.
In memoriam Reverendissimi D.D.
Jacobi Keating Epi. Fernensis: natus anno 1783,
consecratus anno 1819, obiit anno 1849.

religionis et patriae jurum
propugnator strenuus et constans,
Ecclesiam hanc cathedralem
a fundamentis extruxit;
Ecclesiam vero Fernensem legibus, institutis,
moribus, composuit et ornavit.
R. I. P.

Myles Murphy, *suc.* 1850; *ob.* 1856.

Dr. Murphy was born September 8, 1787, at Ballin, Oulart, in the parish of Litter, county Wexford, of Nicholas Murphy and Mary Foley. He was educated in his youth by the Franciscan Friars in their school in Gibson's Lane, Wexford. With him studied three other brothers, intended by their good parents for the Church. The eldest boy joined the insurgents of 1798, and fell by the side of his uncle, the celebrated Father Michael Murphy, in the battle of Arklow. The second died in his 33rd year while engaged as curate in the town of Wexford, revered and lamented by all who knew him. The third (Laurence) served in the diocese of Ossory, and died about the year 1847, a victim to his zeal in ministering to the poor stricken by disease and famine.

On the 5th October, 1804, Myles, the youngest of the brothers, went to Maynooth College, and entered at his own request, being still in his 16th year, the second class of humanity. He took first premium *solus* in rhetoric and philosophy; and in his second year's theology, first premium *solus* in moral, second premium in dogma, his successful rival in dogmatic theology being James M'Hale of Tuam, afterwards P.P. of Castlebar. In the college register, the distribution of prizes for the year 1811, Dr. Murphy's last year is wanting; but we have it on the best authority that he was regarded by his companions as the most talented and distinguished student who entered Maynooth from its foundation in 1795 to the year 1811, when he left college.

He received clerical tonsure in June, 1807, minor orders the next year, subdeaconship in 1809, deaconship in 1810, and priesthood in 1811, as appears from the well kept ordination book of Maynooth. On leaving college, he was appointed by the Most Rev. Dr. Ryan to take charge of the diocesan seminary, then founded in the town of Wexford, near the place on which the new and beautiful Church of the Assumption has been since raised. The present College of St. Peter's was built afterwards under Dr. Murphy's own care, and opened for the reception of students in 1819.

In 1828 Dr. Murphy was chosen Bishop of Ossory, but some of the clergy of that diocese were not pleased with his appointment, and out of respect to their feelings, or from personal motives, he declined the responsibility, even after the Bulls for his consecration had been some time in his hands. He was appointed parish priest of Tintern in 1831, and subsequently Vicar-General. On the demise of Dr. Corrin in 1835, he was named parish priest of Wexford, where, by his uniform kindness and strict attention to duty, he won the affectionate respect and esteem of all classes. On the death of Dr. Keating in 1849, he was unanimously elected Vicar-Capitular, and afterwards all but unanimously recommended for the vacant see, and consecrated on the 10th March, 1850 (See obituary in *Tablet* of 23rd August, 1856).

The good bishop's admirers were not disappointed in his administration, which was firm, impartial, and devoted entirely to the interests of religion. Few, indeed, could be deceived in him who had the pleasure of even a slight acquaintance. In every respect he was the model of a perfect ecclesiastic. His calm countenance, his noble, unaffected deportment, his polite attention to all who approached him, reflected faithfully the inmost feelings of his soul. But though his whole demeanour was marked by meekness, he was firm and uncompromising in the discharge of his duty. Before as well as after his consecration he abstained studiously from interference with political questions, influenced, perhaps by the sad memory of what he had seen in youth, or heard from near relatives. He seemed, indeed, to be over anxious lest any suspicion should fall on himself on account of the well-known traditions of his family. Dr. Murphy attended the National Synod of Thurles in 1850, taking with him as his consulting theologian his present gifted successor in the see of Ferns, Dr. Furlong, then Professor of Divinity in Maynooth College. He also assisted at the Provincial Synod of Dublin of 1853, with Dr. Furlong as consulting theologian. The long and anxious deliberations at these meetings were too great a strain on the energy of a man who had already passed the prime of life, and who for many years had been occupied in very hard missionary duty. Dr. Murphy's health gradually declined from the beginning of 1856, and he died on the 14th of August in that year, in the 69th year of his age. His remains lay exposed in solemn state in the Church of Enniscorthy from Friday until Monday, the 18th of

August, when, after the solemn office and High Mass, celebrated by the Most Rev Dr. Cullen, Archbishop of Dublin, they were deposited in a vault behind the high altar. The obsequies were attended by Most Rev. Dr. Walsh, Bishop of Ossory, Monsignor Yore, V.G., Dublin, and more than a hundred priests, some of whom came from distant dioceses to pay this last tribute of respect.

INSCRIPTION ON BRASS PLATE UNDER DR. MURPHY'S MEMORIAL WINDOW IN ENNISCORTHY CATHEDRAL.

Of your charity pray for the soul of the
Right Rev. Doctor Milesius Murphy. He was
consecrated Bishop of Ferns on March 10th, 1850,
and died on August 13th, 1856, aged 69 years.
His remains were deposited in the chancel near this window.
R. I. P.

We are enabled to give exact copies of all these inscriptions in Enniscorthy Church, through the kindness of the Rev. T. Furlong, Adm., Wexf.

THOMAS FURLONG, *suc.* 1857. *Deus incolumem servet.*

From long and intimate acquaintance with not a few of the distinguished prelates who now rule the Irish Church, we are fully convinced that nothing could give their lordships more pain than complimentary allusion to their prudence, zeal, or success in the ministry. In our notice, therefore, of bishops who are still labouring in God's vineyard, we shall refer only to such facts as are more or less public. and may be mentioned without praise or blame. Thomas Furlong, son of James Furlong and Elizabeth Bent, was born in the parish of Moyglass, barony of Forth, county of Wexford, and baptized on the 4th Feb., 1803. After spending five years in St. Peter's College, Wexford, under the care of his illustrious predecessor in the see of Ferns, he entered Maynooth for logic on Sept. 28, 1819. Having read the usual course of philosophy and theology with distinction, he was elected to the Dunboyne establishment, June, 1824, and ordained priest in the college chapel at Pentecost, 1826, by the Most Rev. Dr. Murray, Archbishop of Dublin. These particulars with some others may be seen in the examination of the Rev. T. Furlong, senior of the Dunboyne class, before the Maynooth Commission, Nov. 2, 1826, *Appendix to Report*, p. 412. From the college calendar it appears that the Rev. Thomas Furlong was appointed junior dean, June 28, 1827; professor of humanity, Feb. 12, 1829, and of rhetoric, Sept. 17, 1834; professor of first year's theology, Sept. 13, 1845, and of second year's, Jan. 20, 1852. He received his Bulls for Ferns at Maynooth College, Feb. 16, 1857, and was consecrated bishop on the 22nd March, 1857, in the cathedral of Enniscorthy by the Most Rev. Dr. Cullen, Archbishop of Dublin, assisted by the bishops of Kildare and Ossory.

To others we must leave the pleasing task of writing the further history of Dr. Furlong's apostolic labours. His family is, we believe, remarkably long lived. His much respected father passed to his reward only about ten years ago. That the son may live to the same old age is, I am sure, the fervent prayer of those who have had at any time the happiness of his lordship's friendship and acquaintance. To the ever faithful people of Wexford we venture to say in all humility, *obey your prelate and be subject to him, for he watches as being to render an account of your souls.*

ADDITIONAL NOTE TO PAGE 43.

Our sincere thanks are due to the Very Rev. William Moran, P.P., Clongeen, County Wexford, for the following particulars: Dr. Sweetman was interred, not in the church, but in the graveyard of Clongeen, along with other members of his family, one of whom, Roger Sweetman, died at the age of 102 years. The tombstone is now level with the ground, and the inscription cannot be easily read:

*Here lies the body of
the Most Rev. Doctor
Nicholas Sweetman, who departed
this life the 19th October, 1786,
aged 86 years, Bishop of Ferns 42.
Requiescat in Pace. Amen*

The stone (without inscription), placed over Dr. Caulfield's grave in the Franciscan Church, Wexford, is now covered by the tiles of the new floor. A mural slab commemorates the date of his appointment as coadjutor, 1782, and his death, 14th Jan, 1814.

COLLECTIONS

ON

IRISH CHURCH HISTORY.

FROM THE MSS. OF THE LATE
VERY REV. LAURENCE F. RENEHAN, D.D.,
President of Maynooth College.

EDITED BY
THE REV. DANIEL M'CARTHY, D.D.,
VICE-PRESIDENT, MAYNOOTH.

VOL. II.
IRISH BISHOPS.

PART II.

DUBLIN:
JAMES DUFFY AND SONS, 15, WELLINGTON QUAY,
AND 22 PATER NOSTER ROW, LONDON.
LONDON: BURNS, OATES, AND CO., 17 PORTMAN STREET.
1874.

PRICE ONE SHILLING AND SIX PENCE.

BISHOPS OF LIMERICK.*

CORNELIUS O'NEILL, *suc*. 1581; *ob*. 1595 (*circiter*).

The successor of Hugh Lacy, deceased in 1580, was Cornelius O'Neill (or Nachten), appointed in 1581. See in *Record*, vol. ii., pp. 22, 23, two letters preserved in the Roman Archives, both from Madrid, dated respectively June 20, 1583, November 16, 1584, signed "*Cornelius Episcopus Limericensis*". From a state paper in the Public Record Office, it appears that Bishop Cornelius was still in Spain in 1591 (not 1597—a misprint in *Record*, *ibid*.). But nothing further is known of his life, or the time or manner of his death. We thought it well to direct attention again to the life of Bishop Cornelius, on account of the doubtful manner in which we spoke of the entry in Lopez, in our note to Dr. Kelly's *Dissertations*, p. 439.

The next Catholic Bishop of Limerick was :—

RICHARD ARTHUR, *suc*. 1623 ; *ob*. 1646.

Richard Arthur was born in the county Cork about 1560, studied in Louvain where he was ordained, and returned to Ireland in 1598. It was a perilous time for a young Catholic priest to enter on his sacred office. For few of his class survived the fiery ordeal which began with the reign of Elizabeth. There was no bishop, at least resident, in the province of Munster, and much of the care of the southern Church

* On the 1st of January, 1874, I sent by post to my printer in Dublin the second Part of this volume, containing about 100 pages. The parcel was detained or destroyed in the Post-office, and never delivered. As I kept no copy of the MS., I could not supply the lost Part. I have been thus obliged to delay the publication, and to change the order of this work.

devolved upon Dr. Arthur, specially after his consecration. From the very beginning he devoted himself with unselfish zeal to the cares of the ministry. Nor were his labours confined to his native province. He preached the word and dispensed the mysteries throughout a great part of Leinster and Connaught; but in Limerick he dwelt chiefly, where he exercised the powers of Vicar Apostolic. When the Queen's death was announced in Ireland, and when the new King was proclaimed, "for whose advent the Catholics had so long sighed", the Rev. Richard Arthur, at the head of the citizens of Limerick, was among the first to celebrate the auspicious change. "With sacred chant and solemn rite he purified the desecrated church of St. Mary, and the other churches within the city".—White's Narrative, Duffy's *Hibernian Magazine*, November, 1848, p. 273.

Dr. Arthur was appointed Bishop of Limerick on the 18th of May, 1620, and consecrated on the 7th of September, 1623, by David Rothe of Ossory, "the Bishop of Cork, and Luke Archer, Abbot of Holy Cross, assisting at the ceremony".*

His episcopate does not seem to have attracted much the attention of our annalists, who hardly allude to his manner of life or his ministry. The only event of public importance with which they connect his name was the rejoicing in honour of the Nuncio Rinuccini, on his first arrival in Limerick, October, 1645. The ceremony was imposing and solemn, second only in splendour to the reception in the glorious city of the Confederation. The venerable bishop, worn out by age and toil, and un-

---

* Duffy's *Hibernian Magazine*, p. 204. It is much to be regretted that the writer quotes his authorities so sparingly. Who was Bishop of Cork in 1623? See *Collections*, vol. I., p. 275.

able to officiate in person, was borne by his attendants to the cathedral porch, whence the clergy, attired in their robes, the various civil and municipal authorities, went out in joyful procession to the gates of the city, to welcome the Pope's representative, and to offer him their humble and grateful homage. The Nuncio himself was so deeply impressed with this manifestation of the people's faith and reverence, that he loves to dwell on the minute details in his letters to Rome. This would seem to have been the last occasion in which Dr. Arthur appeared in public. I find his name to a letter of July 21, 1628, signed by four other bishops (Thomas Dublin, William Cork and Cloyne, Maurice Emly, Boetius Elphin), recommending Malachy Quaely to Killaloe, vacant by the death of Cornelius. On the 20th of July, 1630, he applied to the Holy See for a coadjutor, on the ground that he was old and infirm, being now almost seventy years of age, and exhausted by his labours in the ministry, having spent thirty-two years and more in the most trying times in the city and diocese of Limerick, promoting, according to the best of his ability, the Catholic cause. Wherefore he recommends three priests to the Pope as the fittest persons to assist him in the government of the diocese, with the right of succession. These three were Richard Goold, of the Order of Trinitarians, James Arthur, a Dominican, and Dr. John Creagh, a secular priest. The petition concludes thus:

"By this means, too, an opportunity shall be given to us, who are now hastening to the grave, to atone for the ignorance of our youth, and the offences of our entire life, and to recount all our years in the bitterness of our souls in true sorrow and repentance. And we call God to witness, that in this recommendation we have not been influenced by the prayers of those named, nor by reward (God forbid), nor hope of any temporal advantage or gain, but purely by the motives already specified".*

A like petition was forwarded on July 15, 1632, in favour of the same three priests, signed by John Waring, Dean of Limerick; Philip Hurrow, Rector of St. John's and V.G.; Jordan De Burgo, Archdeacon; Philip Hogan, V.G. and Treasurer; James Galway, P.P. St. Mary's, and V.G.; Revs. William Hibert, John Cantillon, Robert Rudel, James Ling, Edward Fitzgerald, Maurice Nicholls, Cornelius O'Connell, William Houregan, P.P. St. Nicholas; Roger O'Brien, P.P. Killady, and Donatus Hally. To this postulation the bishop subscribed his name, declaring that the facts stated were true and the signatures genuine. No coadjutor was, however, named until 1645, when Dr. O'Dwyer was appointed, with the right of succession.

Dr. Arthur died in Limerick on the 23rd of May, 1646, after a lingering illness, and was buried in St. Mary's Cathedral. John Baptist Rinuccini attended the funeral, and chanted the last prayers over his grave. Taking into account the hard times in which Dr. Arthur lived, his scanty resources, and the pressing wants of his people, he must be reckoned among the best benefactors of his see.

"There are still extant (says White, A.D. 1738) many valuable presents he made to it, viz., in 1624 he gave two plate cruets for wine and water, engraved and partly gilt; in 1625 he gave a large plate-gilt crucifix, hollow inside for relics, nicely engraved, with a pedestal or degrees of plate set with stones, and in the upper cross there is inlaid, in the form of a cross, a very large relic of the Holy Cross of Christ; it was designed to be carried before the bishop. In 1627 he gave a large plate-

* See the original Latin letters in *Record*, vol. ii., pp. 309 ff.

gilt chalice and patena, enamelled, and a plate pax, nicely enamelled, and the enamelled work representing the crucifixion, and the soldier piercing Christ's side with a lance. In 1634 he gave a gilt plate remonstrance for the Blessed Sacrament, supported by four pillars and a crown over it".—White's MS., p. 62.*

A curious note inserted by Dr. Young, Bishop of Limerick, in White's MS. history, may be referred to here :

" I have in my possession a dispensation granted in the forbidden degrees of kindred to Leonard Creagh and Ioan White, in order to be married, which is dated November 6, 1613, and signed Matthew M'Creagh, but the *place* where it is dated is not mentioned, which induces me to suspect that said Matthew Macreagh was the Catholic Bishop of Limerick before Richard Arthur. Said dispensation is written *in Latin*, and the granter says that he grants it by authority vested in him by the Holy See".

Others, deceived by the similarity of names, have identified M. M'Creagh with the ill-famed pluralist, Miler Magrath, Archbishop of Cashel ; but M. Macreagh sat neither in Limerick nor in Cashel : he was Vicar-General of Killaloe for many years, from the close of the sixteenth century until after 1613, and died, as he lived, a simple priest, distinguished for zeal and piety.—See *Relac'on of the Ecclesiastical State in common and particular*, in Fitzgerald's *Declaration*, made on the 24th June, 1613 (MS. T.C.D.).

Bruodin states that M'Creagh was Vicar-General of Killaloe after 1610. He was confessor to John Burk (put to death for the faith in Limerick, A.D. 1610), and wrote an account of that tragic event, the original of which Bruodin held in his own hands.—See

---

* See this extract in Mr. Lenihan's valuable work, *The History of Limerick*, p. 587, where the note added by Dr. Young is ascribed to White himself.

Anatomicum examen Encheridii Apologetici, p. 56, a very curious book, written by Father Cornelius O'Mollony, O.M.

Mr. Lenihan is mistaken, when he says, p. 587, that "the name of Mathew Macrah appears in the list of bishops in White's MSS.". Not in White's MS., but in the addition to it by Dr. Young.

EDMUND O'DWYER, *suc.* 1645; *ob.* 1654.

"On the death of Richard Arthur", says White, "Edmund O'Dwyer was promoted to the See of Limerick, I suppose by the Pope's Nuncio, who was then in Limerick". It is surprising how little White knew of this famous bishop's history. After the words just quoted, he says: "He was one of those who were exempted in the surrender to Ireton. . . Whether he was then executed, or whether he made his escape to foreign countries, has not come to my knowledge". And then is added, in a different hand: "He died in his banishment in Brussels: according to W. Harris on the Irish writers, he wrote two small pieces of poetry, one on the miracles of St. Bridget, the other on the inextinguishable fire of St. Bridget at Kildare".—White, p. 64. In page 62, erased to a great extent, I observe the following sentence, as far as I can judge, in White's own handwriting: "1649. The Most Rev. Edmund O'Dwyer, Bishop of Limerick, died in his banishment at Brussels".

Edmund O'Dwyer was born in the county of Limerick,[*] studied at Rouen first, then at the Sorbonne,[†]

---

[*] Ferrar's *Limerick*, p. 359. Mr. Lenihan's notice of Bishop O'Dwyer is for the most part confessedly taken from the Rev. Mr. Meehan's book on the *Irish Hierarchy*.

[†] Duffy's *Hibernian Magazine*, September, 1863, p. 264. The date 1644,

where he gained the friendship of Dr. Quaely of Tuam, afterwards at Rheims, and finally at Rome, where he was admitted Doctor of Divinity. Soon after he was appointed Procurator and Roman agent of the Irish Bishops, and as such presented the usual report of the state of Dr. Quaely's diocese in Sept., 1634. At his grace's urgent request, he also exerted himself much to procure the appointment of Dr. Kirwan to the See of Killala, which was, however, postponed, in consequence of the opposition made by Dr. Kirwan himself. Dr. O'Dwyer continued to represent the Irish Bishops in the Eternal City until he set out for Ireland, about the end of 1641. On his way he tarried for some months in France, trying to raise men and money for the Irish Confederates. In one of Wadding's letters, dated April 22, 1642, he informs the Cardinal Protector that Sir Edmund is in Paris, and about to leave for Nantes, in Bretagne, whence he will sail to Ireland with a few Irish colonels and captains. And in another letter, written also in April same year, Wadding anticipates that Sir Edmund "is by this time in Ireland, and acting according to the Cardinal's instructions".

Dr. O'Dwyer did not, however, reach the Irish coast as soon as his Roman friends expected. The ship in which he sailed was seized by Turkish pirates, and the crew and passengers taken to Smyrna and sold there as slaves. O'Dwyer was purchased for 200 scudi (crowns) by a French merchant (a Calvinist), who treated him kindly, and promised to set him free at any time on payment of the purchase money with interest. Even this small sum it was not easy

p. 204, *ibid.*, is a misprint for 1634, when the *relatio status* was presented in the name of Dr. O'Quaely. In Dr. Moran's *Memoirs of Dr. Plunket*, p. 385, the report itself may be seen, dated 14th September, 1634.

to procure from his poor countrymen in exile. After a few months he sent an account of his captivity and the required ransom to Rome.*

That Irishmen were often captured at the time by Moorish pirates cannot be doubted. Bruodin states that such was the fate of his friend Stephen Shortall, Abbot of Bective in Meath. Nor did ecclesiastics alone suffer; see account of the capture by the Turks of Edward Plunket, Lord Fingall's son, in *Kilkenny Archæological Journal*, April, 1873.

Wadding appealed in his behalf to the Cardinal Protector, who ordered the ransom to be paid off at once, with sufficient funds to defray the expenses of O'Dwyer's journey to his own country.

He arrived in Ireland about the beginning of 1643, and "saw with his own eyes" the rapid progress of the Confederate movement, in which he was destined to have a leading part afterwards.

This account is taken chiefly from Wadding's letter to the Cardinal Protector, dated October 3, 1642. He tells how "poor Don Dwyer was made a slave by the Turks, taken to Barbary for sale, and bought by a Calvinist merchant of Rochelle, where he remained until the purchase money (300 scudi, including interest) was paid back". He requests the Cardinal to deliver him from this misery, and to send new instructions, Don Dwyer having been obliged to cast into the sea the letters given him formerly. A different version of the whole story may be seen in

---

* The letter, which he wrote to Wadding from Rochelle, August 26, 1642, was first published in the *Record*, vol. ii., p. 365. In it are described minutely his own sufferings while in bondage. He praises the kindness and humanity of the merchant, who paid for his release 200 scudi, "without any security, without any knowledge of the person or character of the captive, or probable hope of being repaid his money";

Duffy's *Hibernian Magazine*, September, 1863, and in Mr. Lenihan's *History of Limerick*, p. 591, according to which it was after O'Dwyer's consecration that he was captured, and further that he was released, not through Wadding and the Cardinal, but through the exertions of a lady who heard accidentally of his servitude, and the cruelty of his master. That our account, though less imaginative and romantic, is the true one, is plain from the letters we have quoted.

Dr. O'Dwyer was not permitted to enjoy rest and peace at home for a long time. In 1644 the Supreme Council, then sitting in Kilkenny, deputed him to proceed to Rome with their petition praying the Holy Father to raise the celebrated Luke Wadding, the very man to whom he owed so many obligations, to the dignity of Cardinal. Engaged in such a cause, he lost no time in repairing to the scene of his former labours; but the Pope died in the meantime, and partly for this reason, but chiefly on account of the active measures taken by Wadding himself to defeat the project, the petition was never presented; nay, it was not heard of by Wadding's own nephew, Father Harold, until he found it among his papers after his death. Wadding acknowledged, however, in a letter, which deserves to be written in letters of gold, his obligation to the Supreme Council, and saw and appreciated the zeal and ability of their agent. He knew his merits from the familiar intercourse of former years, and longed for an opportunity of recommending him for a higher position in the Church. Through his influence chiefly, Dr. O'Dwyer was named Coadjutor of Limerick, with the title of bishop of *Calama in partibus;* and he and his friend Dr. Kirwan were consecrated together, May 7, 1645, in the church of St. Lazare, Paris, by the Bishop of Senlis. There is strong reason to believe that among the priests who assisted at the ceremony was the glorious St. Vincent of Paul, who was the personal friend of Dr. O'Dwyer. And that friendship produced blessed fruits.

In 1646, the priests of the Congregation of the Mission (St. Vincent's) were first sent to Ireland at the earnest request of the Bishop of Limerick. They laboured hard, as Dr. O'Dwyer testifies in a letter to the superior in Paris, to bring sinners to repentance, and to engrave the truths of faith in the hearts of the people. To the children of St. Vincent, he says, he owes his own salvation. " Write to them a word of consolation. I know not under heaven a mission more useful than this of Ireland, for although we had a hundred missioners, the harvest would be still great and the labourers too few".—*Life of St. Vincent*, by Bishop Abelly.

White's statement, that O'Dwyer was appointed through the influence of the Nuncio, is quite groundless, as it is certain, and proved juridically, that the Irish Bishops, without exception, from 1624 to 1646, were nominated by Wadding.

Immediately after their consecration, both prelates, Drs. O'Dwyer and Kirwan, returned to Ireland, and on the death of Dr. Arthur, on the 23rd May, 1646, Dr. O'Dwyer succeeded to the See of Limerick. His history for a long time subsequently, like that of most of his colleagues, is almost entirely and intimately wound up with the struggle of the Confederates. On August 12, 1646, he attended the synod of Waterford, and signed the declaration then issued by the Nuncio against the peace lately concluded between the Earl of Ormonde and the Supreme Council. But this was perhaps the only, and certainly the last occasion on which he joined the Nuncio. On the contrary, when the cessation of arms with Lord Inchiquin was debated in 1648, although the Nuncio protested against it, O'Dwyer boldly put his name at the head of the remonstrance of the Supreme Council. He was one of the three bishops who declared that the treaty with Inchiquin was not the same as that rejected by the Irish Bishops in August, 1648, though the Nuncio based his censures on their identity and on the contumacy manifested by those who now approved the very terms they had rejected with horror before. And he was one of the nine prelates who concluded the peace with Lord Ormonde, and presented him at Kilkenny with the articles of agreement, January 16, 1649, and published a joint pastoral to their flocks on the 18th January, approving that peace, and exhorting all the Catholics to observe it faithfully. He was still not a blind adherent of the peace party, for we find him signing the declaration of the synod of Jamestown in 1650, expressly directed against Ormonde himself.* And though his conduct in supporting the insidious policy of that minister may well be questioned, and even justly, as we think, condemned, it is plain he acted from principle, from a deep sense of duty, not from servile compliance to any earthly power. Hence, long after, when in exile, and even on his death-bed, after experiencing the sad consequences of dissension, he firmly refused to ask for absolution from those censures which, he knew, he could not incur unless guilty of sin and disobedience. If he acted indiscreetly in supporting

* De Burgo's *Hib. Dom.*, pp. 74, 87, 657, 665, 692, 876, 884, 890, 911.

wrong views for a time in the councils of the Confederates, he atoned amply for this fault by his firmness on more trying occasions. When Limerick was besieged by Ireton, the loyal and patriotic bishop made every effort to prevent the mayor and citizens from agreeing to any surrender. He attended the sick and wounded, not only in the hospitals, but even on the very walls of the city.

Archdeacon Lynch's notice of Dr. O'Dwyer is most interesting, and not too highly coloured, notwithstanding the writer's strong prejudice against the Nuncio's policy:

"As to Edmund O'Dwyer, he learned knowledge in Paris, prudence and business habits in Rome, piety in both cities. He was an accomplished Greek and Latin scholar, a graceful poet, a subtle philosopher, a deep divine. Rome knew his worth not by hearsay, but, if I may so speak, by eyesight. He was promoted to the episcopacy not through the recommendations of friends, but through personal merit, for his superiors knew thoroughly his excellent gifts, his habits of study and piety. On his return home he laboured hard for his flock, and was the first to introduce the Fathers of the Mission into Ireland, for the instruction and edification of the young, and for the correction and reformation of the old. Having distinguished himself by his prudence in the government of his diocese, he was elected a member of the Supreme Council of State, and when the Confederation was broken up, he withdrew to his own city of Limerick, and there, during a long siege, encouraged his people to resist the enemy. When at length the city was driven to surrender, his persecutors would not spare his life, nor suffer him to escape. Putting on, therefore, the dress and knapsack of a soldier, he passed through the gates quietly, withdrew from the city, and made his way to Belgium, having suffered all but the bloody death of a martyr".

There is strong reason to believe that large sums of money were offered to him, as we know they were to the Bishop of Emly, to betray the cause of the people. But instead of yielding to fear or corruption, he pronounced sentence of excommunication against all who should advise or promote submission. Unfortunately, however, the spirit of cowardice and treason had seized on many of the leaders, and the ill-fated city was delivered to Ireton. In the capitulation the Bishops of Limerick and Emly, with several patriotic citizens, lay and clerical, were excepted by name from mercy or quarter.*

Bishop O'Brien was hanged on the vigil of All Saints, in Limerick, in 1651. Bishop O'Dwyer put on the knapsack of a private, and marched out of the city in the ranks unnoticed. According to another account, he disguised himself in the dress of a porter, and, carrying a heavy, unsightly load on his back, passed through the files of soldiers. His escape through the many perils that awaited him afterwards, whilst the country was devastated by fire and sword, famine and pestilence, seems almost miraculous, large rewards being offered for his apprehension, and spies tracking his secret haunts. At length he fled to the Continent, about the beginning of 1652, and soon after took up his abode at Brussels, where he died, on the 6th March, 1654†. During his exile the good bishop received but a small share of the consolation and sympathy often so generously bestowed by the Catholics of Belgium and France on

* Borlase's *History*, pp. 358-362. Ferrar's *Limerick*, p. 55. *Columbanus*, p. 169.

† De Burgo (from French), p. 490. See *Record*, vol. ii., p. 366: "He [Dr. O'Dwyer] escaped in the disguise of a soldier, and fled to *France*, where he died in 1654". I have not seen any other authority for saying that Dr. O'Dwyer died in France. See, also, the very interesting memoir of Dr. O'Dwyer, in the *Irish Hierarchy of the Seventeenth Century*, by Rev. Mr. Meehan.

his persecuted countrymen. Dr. O'Dwyer, it was universally known, never applied for absolution, and never confessed himself guilty of disobedience in resisting the Nuncio's censures. For this reason, if we may credit one who is not indeed trustworthy, specially in this matter, some Irish Catholics, moved with too fiery zeal, sought in vain to deprive the bishop of Christian burial, and to exclude his mortal remains from consecrated ground.* These zealots seem to have forgotten that, as bishops were not expressly named in the Nuncio's sentence of excommunication, they could not have been affected by it. A prelate who made such sacrifices in the cause of religion was not likely, through obstinate adhesion to his own views, to lose for ever the only reward for which he struggled earnestly in life and prayed fervently in death.

Dr. Henry Jones, raised by Charles I. to the See of Clogher in 1645, afterwards a rebel, and "scout-master-general" to Cromwell's army (a post, says Harris, not so decent for one of his function), and employed by Lord-Deputy Fleetwood as a spy on the Catholics during the whole period of the usurpation, states that Dr. O'Dwyer returned again to Ireland, and died at home. In a letter to the Lord-Deputy, dated January 23, 1655-6, the ungrateful Jones informs the Lord-Deputy, on the authority of one of his scouts, that Bishop O'Dwyer is now in the Queen's County, after returning from exile; that he had an interview there with one Teig Hennessay, a priest, in which he stated that 5,000 Irish soldiers in Flanders,

* Walsh's *Remonstrance*, p. 591. The writer of the articles in Duffy's *Magazine* on " The Hierarchy of the Seventeenth Century" states the opposition succeeded so far as to prevent our bishop being honoured with a public funeral.

in the service of Spain, were ordered out by the King of Spain to proceed to Ireland under the command of Colonel Murta MacTeig O'Brien, and land in Munster, another smaller force being also ready to join at the same time. Hennessay, he says, mentioned all this in confidence to his informant, and moreover referred him for further particulars to a priest named Duling, on whose report he might implicitly rely.

In another letter to the Lord-Deputy also, dated seven days later, viz. January 30, he repeats the same story, adding that Bishop O'Dwyer had visited within a few weeks, several parts of Leinster, Connaught, and Munster, and was now, at the moment of writing, in Clare; that the said bishop and a priest called Bonaventure M'Loughlin are agents for receiving and circulating intelligence from abroad, and corresponding with the Royalist party. At stated times they meet two other priests from England, sent for the purpose of consulting with the Irish Catholics. If the testimony of this base informer can be admitted at all, it proves, at least, that Dr. O'Dwyer came to Ireland in 1655 or 1656. The story, so far, is not utterly improbable; but we believe there is no other evidence to support it. It is certain that the Cromwellian Government dreaded very much at the time that an effort would be made by the King of Spain to restore Charles. They were fully persuaded, also, that the Irish people would gladly welcome any invading army, to save themselves from an odious usurpation. In the same letters, Jones communicated the startling intelligence that a priest, called Owen O'Quinn, lately came from Spain and proceeded to Scotland, and that another was expected soon, whose arrival might be dreaded even more. Meetings of the Irish were convened by priests in or near Connaught, who were encouraged by the newly-appointed Primate (E. O'Reilly). A fast was lately ordered privately, but kept by all the Irish, such as was observed before the rising of 1641. This fast has now lasted from September till January 30, on three days of the week, and never was there greater rigour, the young and old joining in the most severe penitential exercises. To the fast was united incessant prayer, night and day, that God might at length rescue His faithful people from the cruelty of the Government. Such was the account furnished by Jones, on which, indeed, little reliance can be placed, as it is entirely unsupported by any other evidence. It deserved, however, some mention in connexion with our notice of Dr. O'Dwyer and his times.

JAMES DOWLEY, *suc.* 1677; *ob.* 1685.

The only mention of this bishop in White's MS. is a note, seemingly in a strange hand, under the year 1660, which runs thus: "From the Rev. Jasper White's papers we collect that the Rev. James Dowley was this time (1660) Catholic Bishop of Limerick". The writer, if I mistake not, was Dr. Young; but the inference is not justified by White's words, nor otherwise well founded. There was no Bishop of Limerick in 1660. I find the following heading to a letter dated July 1, 1660, prefixed, with other approbations, to Harold's *Abridgment of Wadding's Annals:* "Eximii D. Jacobi Dulaei, O.M.S.T., Lect. Hiberni, S. Theologiae Doctoris Paris., Protonotarii Apostol., quondam Vic. Gen. Dioces. Lim., et Fr. Min. in utraque Momonia Judic. Conserv., nunc

Collegii Neophytorum S. Mariae Montium in Urbe Rectoris, Epistola ad auctorem, Julii ima, 1660". No doubt this is the same James Dowley who was Vicar-General of Limerick in 1653, Vicar-Apostolic in 1669, recommended to the vacant see by the Council of Dublin 1670, and made bishop in 1677. He was appointed on 4th of March, 1677, and consecrated on the 19th of August following, by Dr. Brennan, Archbishop of Cashel, assisted by the Bishops of Cork and Ossory.—*Record*, ii. p. 867.

He had been in 1660, and for some time before, at the head of the College for Catechumens in Rome. In 1656 he was first named Vicar-Apostolic of Limerick, but did not accept that office until his second appointment by decree of January 11, 1669. On this occasion he wrote the following letter:

"Paris, August 23, 1669.

"MOST ILLUSTRIOUS AND REVEREND LORD,—I return exceeding thanks to your Excellency for my election in the last Congregation (through your solicitude and care) as Vicar-General of Limerick, and I also find that it is your intention to exalt me, though still unworthy, to a still higher dignity. To all the appointment of Dr. Plunket is most pleasing, and I doubt not but it will be agreeable to the government, to the secular clergy, and to the nobility; and all this we owe to your Excellency. We shall soon return to our country, when I shall send an account of the flock committed to my care.

"JAMES DOWLEY.

"To the Archbishop of Caesarea".

It has been fairly inferred from Dr. Plunket's letter of 28th September, 1671 (*Dr. Plunket's Life by Dr. Moran*), "I sent another letter to Dr. Dowley, Bishop of Limerick", that Dr. Dowley had been consecrated before that date (Mr. Lenihan's *History*, p. 612); but the very same letter is quoted again in

p. 145 (Dr. Moran's *Memoir of O. Plunket*), without the word "bishop": "I sent another parcel of them to Dr. Dowley, of Limerick". Certain it is that Dr. Dowley was not consecrated before 1677. I have not been able to ascertain as yet the exact date of Dr. Dowley's death. He had the leave of the Government in September, 1680, "to remain in Ireland on account of his great age and infirmities" (Dr. Brennan's letter in Dr. Moran's *Plunket*, p. 279). This permission was still continued in May, 1682. His latest ordination in the Government Registry of 1704 is in 1684, when he ordained at Limerick the Rev. Thady M'Namara, P.P. of St. Peter's, Cork. Dr. John Stritch appeared as Procurator of the *Chapter of Limerick* at the Provincial Synod held at Cashel October 6, 1685. At this date, therefore, the See of Limerick was vacant, and the bishop must have died at the close of 1684 or beginning of 1685.

JOHN MOLONY, *suc.* 1688; *ob.* 1702.

"1687. On the 4th October, being St. Francis's day, the Franciscan Fryars possessed themselves of their own church in the Abby; it was consecrated by the Rev. John Molony, Bishop of Killaloe [Limerick], who had the administration of Limerick [Killaloe], there being no Catholic Bishop of Limerick [Killaloe] at the time. The bishop said the first Mass in it, and the Rev. Jasper White said the second Mass. The Fryars now but rented this church from the Englishman who held it, and who was John Perry, lieutenant of a foot company" (ancestor to Lord Perry).

This is the only notice White has of Dr. Molony, and even in this the names of Killaloe and Limerick (as copied above) are strangely confused in the MS. as it stands at present. The corrections in brackets are clearly the work of a copyist, who did not know when Dr. Molony was made Bishop of Limerick, and wrongly assumed that he had been translated some time before that ceremony. The changes, indeed, in the above extract destroy the sense, for it would be unmeaning to state that Dr. Molony officiated solemnly in *Limerick,* " there being no Catholic Bishop in *Killaloe*". The narrative is clear and easily understood, if we read : Dr. Molony, Bishop of Killaloe, solemnly dedicated the church of the Franciscans in Limerick, "there being then no Bishop of Limerick".

Dr. John Molony, descended of the old and honoured family of Kiltanon, was born in the county Clare, in the year 1617. He studied and taught theology in the College of St. Sulpice, and took his degree of D.D. in the University of Sorbonne. Afterwards he served at the Court of the exiled royal family of England, then as Canon of Rouen, whence he was promoted in May, 1671, to the See of Killaloe.—See the postulation in his favour signed by the Council of Dublin, 1670, in Dr. Moran's most valuable *Memoir of O. Plunket,* p. 124, and Dr. Molony's letter, *ibid.,* p. 38. He did not, however, return immediately to Ireland, though urged to do so, hoping to found a new college for the education of the Irish clergy before leaving Paris.

Primate Plunket insisted strongly on the necessity of his return in a letter to the Nuncio, 20th January, 1672 :

" Dr. O'Molony, of Killaloe, wrote to me about the dread he has of Ormonde and his satellites. But I pray you to write to him to come to his diocese as soon as possible, and without delay, for I spoke about the matter to the Viceroy, and he replied, that having no royal order against him, he would not, on account of the enmity of an individual, exclude from the kingdom the subjects of his Majesty. Whilst we have the present Viceroy, Dr. Molony need not hesitate to come; and let him not wait looking for the formation of colleges by the French King. This is a difficult matter, which would require a length of time, and the success of which is very dubious".

The Nuncio himself wrote to the same effect, and Dr. Molony came to his diocese at the end of 1672. But the very next year he went back to Paris, at the unanimous request of the Irish Bishops to ask the support of the French King and his minister for his own favourite project—the establishment of an Irish ecclesiastical college. Primate Plunket, who had been so much opposed to any further delay abroad, wrote now in a different spirit to the Cardinal Protector, 14th March, 1673:

"All the prelates of this kingdom have subscribed an authorization for the Bishop of Killaloe to proceed to Paris, and procure for us a college; and it is certain that no one could be selected better suited to treat this matter, for he is a great friend of the Archbishop of Paris and of the Ambassador of the King of France in London, and there are strong reasons and just grounds for hoping that the college will be founded. If so, it will be a great seminary for the missions of this kingdom. . . . It is certain that the Bishop of Killaloe will do more good by procuring for us that college, than he would did he remain in his diocese during his whole lifetime".

The college was opened not many years after, and endowed by the Bishop of Killaloe, who is justly reputed its founder. He was back again in Ireland in 1674, striving zealously for the salvation of souls. But the history of his further labours belongs properly to the Diocese of Killaloe, where his name is best remembered. The reader will find in Dr. Moran's *Memoir*, pp. 33, 154, 218, 225, 233, and 279, many interesting facts recorded of the life of this distinguished prelate. His services in reconciling

Drs. Plunket and Talbot are specially deserving of notice. From the letter of Dr. Brennan, Archbishop of Cashel, dated 12th September, 1680, we learn that the Bishop of Killaloe " was not then in his own district, but elsewhere; he is in strict concealment; and justly so, for our enemies bear him great ill-will, and speak violently against him". He left Ireland soon after, as we find him acting as coadjutor to the Bishop of Rouen in 1682. The date of his translation to Limerick is uncertain, but it could not have been before the end of 1688, for on the 28th October, that year, Innocent XI. wrote to King James, saying that in the next consistory he would promote the Bishop of Clogher to Meath, and the Bishop of Killaloe to Limerick (Theiner MS.).

It would seem that Dr. Molony did not remain long in Limerick after his translation. I think it likely that he left Ireland, or rather was forced to leave, in April, 1689, " an immense number of Irish secular priests having then landed in France". When his Vicar-General, the Rev. James Stritch, had been proposed for the See of Emly by King James, Jan. 31, 1693, it was urged in his favour that the diocese, though small, needed much " the comfort of a bishop, the more so as it adjoins Limerick, the bishop of which *never* resided there".*

The petition of the Irish Bishops to Pope Innocent XII., dated St. Germain, February 18, 1692, is signed by " *Limericensis Eps. Administrator Laonensis*", as well as their joint letter of thanksgiving, December 8, 1692, for the bill of exchange for 300 crowns, which the Pope sent for their relief. Dr. Molony spent the last four years of his life in the

* See Dr. Moran's *Plunket*, and Mr. Lenihan's *History of Limerick*, pp. 220, 18 ff., who used a faulty copy of the epitaph (*infra*).

Sulpician house at Issy, near Paris, where he died on the 3rd of September, 1702, in the 85th year of his age. On July 13th, 1835, I [L. F. R.] transcribed the following epitaph from a marble slab fixed in the side wall of the Irish College, Paris, whither it had been removed from the Lombards:

"D. O. M.

"Illustrissimus et Reverendissimus Joannes O'Molony ex antiquissima inter Hibernos familia ortus, Parisiis ab adolescentia educatus, et sacrae Facultatis Parisiensis Doctor, ex canonico Rothomagensi factus primum Episcopus Laonensis, sui nominis et familiae tertius, deinde Episcopus Limericensis et Administrator Laonensis, Catholicae religionis et patriae ardens zelator, propterea ab hereticis ad necem saepe quaesitus, tandem ad Parisias re [diens] exul, huic collegio 300 libellas Turonensis annui redditus, praeter 1,200 libellas in constructionem hujus sacelli semel donatas, ex corde legavit. Obiit die tertia Septembris, anno Domini 1702, aetatis suae 85. R.I.P"

CORNELIUS O'KEEFFE, *suc.* 1720; *ob.* 1737.

After Limerick had been left without a bishop for many years (White is mistaken in saying there was no Catholic Bishop since Cromwell's time—see his *Annals*, under the year 1737, p. 87), the Holy Father, hoping that the fiery persecution which had raged hitherto was now about to cease, or at least that a bishop's life would be less exposed to danger, resolved to promote the Rev. Cornelius O'Keeffe to the vacant see. Dr. O'Keeffe was born in the county of Cork, of the respectable family of the O'Keeffes of Glan-na-Phricane, and applied himself with diligence and success to ecclesiastical study in the college of Toulouse. At the end of his course he was honoured with the degree of Doctor of Divinity, and soon after provided with a benefice in the Diocese of Nantes.

From this secure retreat Pope Clement XI. called him to a position of great peril, and in the year 1720 Dr. O'Keeffe took possession of the See of Limerick. He resolved at once to reform those abuses that had crept in while there was no bishop. For this purpose he drew up and published, on the 20th June, 1721, an excellent body of laws, in which, among many other useful measures of reform, he forbade, under pain of suspension *ipso facto*, all those priests from saying Mass, who, without any previous clerical training, had received orders, and all parish priests from giving them an opportunity of saying Mass after the Feast of St. John Baptist; he also commanded all such priests, under the same penalty, to go before the 29th of September following to some foreign college, to be properly instructed for the sacred ministry.

In 1726 the Mayor of Limerick, Thomas Pierse, committed to gaol one, probably, of this illiterate and now idle class, the Rev. Timothy Ryan, an irregular, " and I fancy (says White), an excommunicated priest", for the legal crime of uniting in marriage a Protestant and Catholic. Ryan was tried for this offence at the next assizes, condemned, and executed at Gallows Green. The Act under which he was accused and sentenced only passed that very year, 1726, and he was the first victim that suffered the extreme penalty of the law for this new crime.

About this time the good bishop was much annoyed with disputes in St. Mary's Parish. The Rev. Wm. Ryan, the excellent parish priest, gave up practically the administration to the Rev. Richard Hennessy, of the Diocese of Cork. After about twelve months' service, some words of wholesome advice which dropped from Hennessy in public offended his flock, and he was finally obliged to retire in 1725, in obedience to the command of the bishop, who could not resist any longer the violence of the people. Hennessy started for Brussels, and through the Internuncio there procured a Bull restoring him to the parish, and appointing him Dean of the diocese. He returned home in 1728, but during his absence the people of St. Mary's rose also against his successor, the Rev. Timothy Sheehan, who thought it prudent to withdraw altogether in 1727. To him succeeded the Rev. Matthew Geeran, a great favourite with the entire parish; so attached, indeed, was the flock to him, that when Hennessy returned, they objected to the removal of Geeran, and Hennessy, though supported by a Papal Bull and all the authority of the bishop, did not get possession of the church until the 22nd of April, 1730, when by a compromise it was arranged that Geeran should serve as coadjutor, and receive one-third of the revenues; the same rule to hold for every future parish priest until Geeran's demise or promotion.

The attachment of the people to Geeran seems to have been as ill-advised as their dislike to Hennessy. In 1731, Mr. John Flynn and Mr. Darby Flannedy appeared before Dr. O'Keeffe, and brought a grave charge against Geeran. From conscious guilt, or unwillingness to appear in public with a tainted character, he fled from the city, with a resolve never to return; "but meeting", says White, "accidentally with Dr. Lloyd, the Bishop of Killaloe, of whose diocese he was a native, he was prevailed upon to return back to Limerick and vindicate his character. For this purpose he instituted a suit against Flynn and Flannedy, in the Protestant Bishop's court, for defamation. They, on the other hand, brought an action against him for the very offence with which they had charged him before Dr. O'Keeffe. These suits were prosecuted for a long time with great scandal. The result was that Dr. O'Keeffe suspended Geeran and deprived him of the curacy of St. Mary's".

In 1733, the vacant places in the chapter were filled up. Among the newly-appointed canons of the Cathedral the most distinguished were the Revs. Eugene O'Sullivan, Patrick Scanlan, Walter Bourke, Robert Hayes, Edward O'Brien, Luke Collins, and James Barry.

Dr. O'Keeffe began now to prepare for a long, and in those days perilous, journey. He found it necessary to make some provision for the wants of the Irish Mission, and for this purpose resolved to go to Paris. Before leaving his diocese he revoked the vicarial powers he had conferred on the Rev. Dr. T. Begley, parish priest of Newcastle; and on the 10th of January, 1733-4, appointed the Rev. J. Leahy, D.D., of Poitiers, parish priest of St. John's and precentor of the chapter, and Dean Richard Hennessy, parish priest of St. Mary's, conjointly Vicars-General of the diocese. He then set out for Paris, and lodged a sum of money in the Seminaire des Irlandais (not in the College of the Lombards, as White says), amply sufficient (as he then thought) for the maintenance in all future time of three students. Candidates for these bursaries should avow their intention of studying for the Church; they should be descended of the O'Keeffes of Glean-na-Prichane (Glenville), and be nominated by the Bishop of Limerick *or* by the Bishop of Cork. This little disjunctive "*or*" led to a serious dispute between Dr. Lacey, the next Bishop of Limerick, and Dr. Walsh of Cork, the former claiming priority because the fund was given by his predecessor, and the right of nomination granted to him in the first place; the latter contending that, as the O'Keeffe family belonged to his diocese, he had the exclusive right of selecting from their descendants candidates, who should not be promoted to orders without his permission. The Paris tribunals decided in favour of the Bishop of Limerick.

During the absence of the bishop the new vicars were not inactive. Dr. Leahy was scrupulously exact in conforming in all respects to the canons of the Church. Hence, dreading lest his appointment in 1730 to St. John's Parish might be questioned, as it formerly belonged to the canons regular of St. Augustine, he obtained, for greater security, Bulls from Rome, confirming him in the parish, and took formal possession again on the 8th March, 1733-4. White observes that this precaution was not needed, because a decree was obtained from the Holy See enacting that the canons regular should make no further claim to any other parishes than those they were then possessed of, until religion should be established on its ancient footing in Ireland. The vicars corrected many abuses with a firm hand. They also made some important changes, but what excited most attention was the expulsion of the parish priest of Kratlo, and of another parish priest, who appealed to the Primate, Dr. Hugh M'Mahon. The vicars, Leahy and Hennessy, refused to recognize any primatial jurisdiction over them, and claimed the protection of the Nuncio. The decision was in favour of the vicars, for in a letter, dated Brussels, August 4, 1736, the Nuncio approved their conduct, and recommended the same course whenever the Primate should interfere in future, until the question of his authority was finally settled one way or the other by the Holy See.

Soon after Dr. O'Keeffe's return to Limerick, he had to settle another suit, which had been commenced before his departure for Paris. Some hermits of St. Augustine came to Limerick and opened a chapel. The Dominicans and Franciscans, previously established there, were displeased with the admission of a new order, which deprived themselves of their scanty means of support. On the 14th Jan., 1733-4, they besought Dr. O'Keeffe to institute an inquiry for the purpose of ascertaining whether the hermits of St. Augustine could prove that they had an establishment formerly in the city. They requested that the inquiry should also extend to the Carmelites and Capuchins. It was plain, they urged, from the Bulls of several Pontiffs, that no new order could be introduced without the sanction of Rome. The case having been put off during the bishop's absence, was now brought forward again, on the 13th September, 1735. The bishop called on the hermits for proof of their claim, appointed a day for the investigation in the Franciscan convent, and promised to hear both sides impartially. Attended by his vicars and the secular clergy of the city, he held his court on the 26th September the same year, then on the 28th November, the 5th and 12th of December, and finally on the 2nd of January, 1735-6, when he pronounced sentence as follows:

"We declare and decide that the brothers of the Order of

the Hermits of St. Augustine never had any monastery, convent, or foundation in the city of Limerick, and, *therefore*, that they have no right or title to dwell in that city, under any pretext, since through this entire kingdom those friars alone are admitted into any cities, towns, or hamlets whose order had convents there before: wherefore we command the Rev. Ff. Edward Durkan and Nich. O'Brien, hermits of the said order, under pain of suspension *ipso facto incurrendae*, not to celebrate Mass or administer any sacrament, and not to hold any chapel for the performance of the Divine mysteries, within this city or diocese, except where they have had convents before; and further, that within twenty days they depart from this city of Limerick.

" Given in the place of our refuge, under our sign and seal, this 2nd day of January, 1735-6.

"✠ Cornelius O'Keeffe, Lim. Ep."

To this decision the Hermits did not tamely submit. They appealed first to the Archbishop of Cashel (Christ. Butler), then to the Primate at Armagh. The other Orders refused to acknowledge any primatial jurisdiction, and sought the protection of the Congregation de Propaganda Fide. But notwithstanding this appeal to Rome, the Primate (Dr. Hugh M'Mahon) insisted on his right to redress the wrongs of the Hermits, and appointed a commissary, who pronounced rather hastily in favour of the Augustinians, who opened their chapel again, and administered the sacraments publicly. But the Hermits did not rely entirely on the Primate's good-will or authority. They procured also a declaration from Rome, suspending all sentences against them *usque ad exitum causae*. How the cause did end finally does not appear. White, from whose *Annals* we have taken these particulars, merely tells us that the Augustinians enjoyed all the freedom of other religious down to the year 1755, when he wrote his narrative.

On February 17, 1735-6, about a year before his death, Dr. O'Keeffe published laws for the Dean and Chapter of Limerick, establishing obedience and union, and extending as far as he could their privileges. In the Appendix will be found the text of these constitutions, or a faithful summary. They prove him a learned, zealous, and prudent prelate. Having governed the diocese for seventeen years wisely, and reformed many of the abuses which grew up before his time, he departed this life on the 4th of May, 1737, amidst the fervent prayers of his people. That he conferred many benefits on his diocese by his exemplary piety, by his untiring labours, and by his wise legislation, is indisputable. The only fault that even his worst enemies could lay to his charge, and it is one that shows a good and tender heart, though it leads to evils of great magnitude, is that he was too indulgent, too much inclined to forgive and forget public wrongs, when it was his duty to punish them. "He was accused", says White, " of being too condescending to the entreaties of his acquaintances, and of being prevailed on at times by them to impose hands on candidates unfit for the holy ministry".

Among the Irish MSS. left by the late Right Rev. John Murphy, of Cork, to Maynooth College Library, there are several poems of merit on Bishop O'Keeffe and his family; but they throw no light whatever on the bishop's private life.

ROBERT LACY, *suc.* 1737; *ob.* 1759.

As soon as the funeral rites of the late bishop had been celebrated with becoming solemnity, Dr. Pierse

Creagh assembled the chapter. The canons met on the 9th of May, and elected Dr. John Leahy, V.G. and P.P. of St. John's, and Dr. John Begley, V.G. and P.P. of Newcastle, conjointly as Vicars-Capitular. The choice was approved and confirmed by Dr. C. Butler, Archbishop of Cashel. The formula of election, brief and simple as it well could be, runs thus:— "Nos infrascripti in pleno capitulo congregati, subscribimus, approbamus, et eligimus vicarios capituli Rev. Dom. Joannem Leahy et Rev. Dom. Joannem Begley, hac die 9ª Maii, anno 1737"; and then follow the signatures of P. Creagh, Decanus, and ten other canons, with their bare names, without title or residence, etc.

Immediately after the election, the members of the chapter went to the church of St. Mary's, to name candidates for the vacant bishopric. They thought proper "to elect and postulate these three, namely, Dr. J. Leahy, Vic. Cap. and P.P. of St. John's; Dr. Pierse Creagh, Dean and P.P. of St. Mary's; and Dr. Robert Lacy, a native of the diocese, then superior of the Irish College at Bordeaux". This postulation was at once despatched to Rome. On the evening of the very same day, the greater part of the chapter and of the clergy of the diocese held a private meeting, at which it was resolved to petition the Holy See in favour of Dr. Lacy. The prayer of the clergy was granted at Rome. Dr. Lacy was appointed bishop by Pope Clement XII., and consecrated on February 23, 1737-8, at Bordeaux, by the Most Rev. Francis Mirabau, Archbishop of that city. The new bishop arrived in Limerick towards the end of September, 1738.

Whatever may be said of the charge against his

predecessor of promoting untried and untrained candidates to holy orders, Dr. Lacy resolved from the outset not to expose himself to any such imputation. He abolished, as far as he could, the old and bad practice of ordaining young men before they had received a full knowledge of the duties of the clerical state. He sent all his students to foreign colleges to be trained in the spirit of their calling before ordination. During an administration of twenty-one years he imposed hands on but one of his own subjects—the celebrated James White, the compiler of the *Annals* which we quote so often. In his case the bishop had the highest testimonials, and few ecclesiastics proved themselves more deserving of the confidence of their superiors, or honourable mention in the history of the city and see of Limerick. The Rev. James White returned home in 1736, a sub-deacon, from the college of Salamanca, where he had studied six years. Though not of age for priesthood at the end of his course, he was obliged to leave college, no student being allowed by the rules of the house to remain longer than six years. He was ordained deacon on Wednesday, the 20th December, 1738, and priest on the 23rd.

The parish of St. Mary's gave almost as much trouble to Dr. Lacy as to Dr. O'Keeffe, though in a different way. On the death of Dean Hennessy, July 1, 1736, Dr. Pierse Creagh was appointed, by authority from Rome, Dean and P.P. of St. Mary's. He had only returned from the Eternal City the preceding year, bringing with him a Bull for the archdeaconry of Limerick and the parish of St. Michael's, of which he took possession in due form on the 21st September, 1735. Shortly after his promotion to the deanery, he was appointed Bishop of Waterford, and the vacant deanery, with the parish of St. Mary's, was conferred by Papal Bull on Dr. John Creagh. To this arrangement Dr. Lacy objected, claiming to himself the right of disposing of the parish. The Cardinal Protector of Ireland, Cardinal Corsini, on being appealed to by Dr. John Creagh, wrote to the bishop, suggesting a compromise. Dr. Creagh was to retain his title of Dean, and get the parishes of Newcastle and Monaghea in lieu of St. Mary's. This proposal did not please the dean, who insisted on his right to St. Mary's, and relied on the validity of the collation by virtue of the grant from Rome. He got personal possession of the parish from Dr. Patrick M'Donagh, Bishop of Killaloe, as the delegate of the Holy See, and he would not give it up without a formal decision of the Roman Court. The whole question at issue seemed to turn on one point, whether the deanery and St. Michael's parish were united by long usage. On the bishop's side witnesses came forward to prove that the dean and parish priest of St. Mary's were, within their recollection, different persons. On the dean's part it was urged that for at least half a century the parish was never separated from the deanery. "The Court of Rome", says White, " which was intent on making good its grant of the parish of St. Mary to Dr. J. Creagh, as it alleged that he was the third person to whom the Court granted the parish, as annexed to the deanery—first, to R. Hennessy; second, to Dr. P. Creagh; and now, to Dr. J. Creagh; consequently, that there was prescription in favour of the Court's grant; and upon this footing the Congregation de Propaganda Fide gave a decree in favour of Dr. J. Creagh, ratifying thereby the Bull for the deanery and the parish of St. Mary annexed thereto".

After this decision, Dr. Creagh took quiet possession of St. Mary's, but a new difficulty arose immediately. He claimed, as appurtenances to St. Mary's, the districts comprised in the parishes of St. Nicholas and St. Francis (the Abbey of), and on the 24th of September, 1747, cited the pastors of these two parishes to appear before the Propaganda within two months. The dispute was thus referred to Rome, and tried there. Dr. Creagh pleaded that these parishes were always under the care of the priests of St. Mary's, and supported this plea by the sworn testimony of twelve of the oldest and most respectable householders in the city of Limerick. The Rev. Michael M'Mahon, one of his opponents, produced a Papal Bull, dated December 9, 1741, granting him the parish of St. Nicholas.

"I, James White, appealed to the collation which Dr. Lacy gave me of the Abbey in 1745, at the presentation of Dr. J. Leahy, and to prove that said Leahy had the right of presentation I got it attested by different people, particularly the inhabitants of the Abbey, that the said Abbey belonged by right to the canons regular, and consequently must be of the annexes of St. John's Parish, which belonged to the said canons, and for which Dr. Leahy had Bulls, with all its annexes; that the Protestant proprietor of the forfeited estates of said canons owned also the Abbey, whose privileges he supports; that in the Protestant Church (which follows the rules that existed before the change) the Abbey never belonged to St. Mary's, nor do its inhabitants ever pay the Protestant minister any tithes, perquisites for marrying, christening, etc.; and that said Abbey in no wise belongs to the city, or is in any way subject to its jurisdiction, but to the county at large".

Having considered the whole subject maturely, the

Propaganda commissioned Dr. C. Butler, Archbishop of Cashel, and Dr. Killikelly, Bishop of Kilfenora, to examine the witnesses in Limerick. Dr. Butler delegated his vicars-general, Laurence Ryan and Daniel Kearney, both doctors of Sorbonne, to appear in his stead. They and the litigants, with Dr. Lacy, met in Limerick on November 15, 1749, but before any discussion a compromise was effected. Messrs. M'Mahon and White consented to serve as coadjutors to Dr. Creagh, M'Mahon receiving a third of the emoluments of both parishes (St. Mary's and St. Nicholas's), and White getting all the revenues of the Abbey.

Not many years after, another more distressing controversy tried the vigilance, zeal, and temper of our worthy bishop. In 1728 the Rev. Patrick Scanlan was appointed parish priest of St. Munchin's, and for a long time displayed much earnestness and seeming propriety of conduct. But in 1754 a kind brother priest informed him, in the most discreet way, of injurious reports affecting his character, and warned him of his danger to no purpose. These rumours soon reached the bishop, who used every exertion to correct the offender by private remonstrance. But all in vain. Scanlan affected to despise the charges, although they were made publicly. He was at length cited by the bishop to appear before him on 13th February, 1754–5, and after a week's examination and the depositions of several witnesses, he was suspended for a year. Against this sentence he appealed, first to the Archbishop of Cashel, on 10th March, and as his Grace did not decide immediately, afterwards to the Primate of Armagh, "cujus jurisdictio", says White, "in hac provincia Momoniae non admittitur et suffulti sumus majorum consuetudine, et subsequenti epistola D'omini Nuncii, data Bruxellis 4ª Aug. 1736". Scanlan, however, did not notify his appeal to the Primate until the 28th June, the very day that Dr. Nicholas Madget, Bishop of Kerry, and Dr James Heynes, Parish Priest of Cullen, came to Limerick as Dr. Butler's commissioners, to hold an inquiry. On the morning of that day he left town to bring his case before the Primate. Nothing could be well done in his absence, and the Archbishop cited him soon after to St. John's Church, Limerick. Accordingly, on the 18th September, 1755, Dr. James Butler and Dr. Heynes, Dr. Lacy and Dr. Daniel Kearney, his vicar, Dr. J. Creagh, dean, James White, secretary, and the accused Scanlan, came together. The meeting was again fruitless, because Scanlan denied the competency of the Archbishop of Cashel to decide the case at all after it had been referred to Armagh. These delays Dr. Lacy strongly protested against, knowing the evils that were increasing every day; he made, therefore, a visitation of St. Munchin's, and publicly read the charges against Scanlan, who gave no answer, but entered another appeal to the Nuncio. The suspensions, he insisted, were informal and of no effect, and he continued to celebrate, although his church was under interdict. Yet he was supported by a violent mob, who even insulted the bishop within the sanctuary.

Though all the appeals made by Scanlan were informal, and of no effect whatever, still Dr. Lacy wrote a full account of the case to the Archbishops of Cashel and Armagh and to the Nuncio. This step brought the long list of appeals to an issue. The

Nuncio delegated the Archbishop of Cashel to examine the whole case, and his Grace advised all parties concerned of this decree. Dr. Butler and Dr. Lacy met at Hospital on the 25th August, 1756, when Scanlan put in a written protest against the authority of both the bishop and archbishop. The moment the archbishop saw this paper he sent it off to the Nuncio, who commissioned him, in turn, to excommunicate by name the appellant for formal disobedience. The archbishop came back again to Limerick on December 4th, cited the accused to appear before him in St. Mary's Chapel, and after reading his commission and explaining its nature and the extent of his powers, warmly exhorted him to make peace and submit to the authority of his bishop. Finding all entreaty fruitless, he pronounced the fatal sentence as directed. As soon as Scanlan heard the last words condemning him, he gave a written act of submission on 4th December, as follows :

"By the commands of James Butler, representative of the Primate of Munster, the Right Rev. Christ. Butler, and delegate from His Excellency the Nuncio at Brussels, I, Patrick Scanlan, at the church of St. Mary's, this 4th day of December, 1756, do submit freely of myself to the said Nuncio's decree, and to my superior, Dr. Robert Lacy, of Limerick, being commanded thereto by the Nuncio; and I hereby do promise perfect obedience to my superior and his successors, and will use my utmost efforts to reform and bring back to obedience all who adhered to me in my mistaken proceedings, and I will make the clearest declaration to this effect for the three subsecutive festivals in the parish church of St. Munchin's, the key of which, and all other things thereunto belonging, I promise to give up to my said Ordinary. Dated the day and year above mentioned, and also in the chapel above mentioned.

"PATRICK SCANLAN".

Every word of what he promised he fulfilled to the letter. The keys of the church and sacred vessels he gave up immediately, and on the next Sunday made an humble act of submission from the altar of St. Munchin's.

Dr. Butler now proposed to execute the other part of the Nuncio's commission, and on the 23rd May, 1757, opened the court in the chapel of St. Patrick's, near Limerick. Three officials were appointed— Very Rev. Daniel Kearney, by the archbishop; Rev. James White, by Dr. Lacy; and Rev. Michael Hoare, ex-prov. of Dominicans, by and for the accused. On the 17th June the archbishop pronounced the final decision, that the appeals were frivolous, and the censures just and valid. Despite all his promises, Scanlan entered a new and final appeal to a Congregation of Bishops and Regulars in Rome. Of the whole proceedings a full account was transmitted to the Nuncio by the archbishop. On July 12th, 1757, the Nuncio, in reply, ordered the sentence already passed to be carried into effect forthwith, promising, at the same time, to report all the facts of the case in Rome. Thus ended this sad controversy, which gave much disedification, and caused the good bishop more bitter regret than any event of his life.

Our object in referring to it is not to revive a long-forgotten scandal, but to illustrate the discipline of the Irish Church at a dark period, and to show the firmness of Dr. Lacy in the most trying circumstances. Dr. Daly, Bishop of Kilfenora, appreciating the high qualities of our good prelate, appointed him, with the sanction of the Holy See, administrator of Kilfenora, whilst he himself continued until his death in 1750 to reside at Tournay, his health and his scanty means not permitting a closer attention to the wants of his diocese.

Much had been done, as we have seen, by Dr. O'Keeffe to improve the government of the clergy and people under his care, and all his reforms were carried out by Dr. Lacy, who embodied them in a code of laws, of which we give a brief account in the appendix. Some of the most useful of these decrees, such as that commanding the publication of the banns, were openly violated by a Franciscan friar, and the Bishop found it necessary to order a sentence of excommunication against him to be read publicly in all the chapels of the diocese on the 16th October, 1748, and to proclaim the same penalty against all priests who would henceforth marry any but their own parishioners, or assist at, encourage, or witness any such marriage. Many other useful measures were also adopted by Dr. Lacy himself for the direction of the clergy. These were at first proposed and approved at the conference of the decanate of Adare on the 9th April, 1752, and on the 13th were discussed and received by the conference of the deanery of Limerick, and afterwards by the other two deaneries. Of these either the text or a faithful outline is inserted also in the appendix. They illustrate the discipline of the Irish Church at an eventful crisis, and show that her rulers were men of learning, piety, and prudence in the most trying times.

Dr. Lacy escaped the rigorous search made for priests and bishops during the short but relentless persecution of 1744-5. Soon after he saw that same religion, then so lowly and despised, assume a higher status. New churches were built throughout the diocese. In Limerick itself there were two chapels for the small one which was used by the people of St. Mary's and St. Munchin's before. During his time the old ruin outside Thomond Gate was entirely abandoned, and the church of St. Munchin's opened and solemnly dedicated. The poor people of St. Mary's met to celebrate the sacred mysteries in thatched cabins, store-houses, etc., until 1749, when their new chapel, which, they boasted, was ninety feet long—one of the largest then in the province— was completed. St. John's new chapel was built by Dr. Leahy, V.G., before his death in 1754.

Thus the city of Limerick, which, at the bishop's accession, had scarcely one parochial church of any kind, was, before many years, well supplied with at least large and commodious houses for public worship. And he lived to see even more important changes in the relation of the Church to the State. He saw in 1757 Catholics received into the public service without being obliged to abjure their faith. He saw them solicited in 1759 to enter the army and navy with a promise of freedom of conscience. He saw, in short, the bigotry and intolerance that prevailed even during his own administration, and often made his life insecure, disappear suddenly and almost entirely before his death.

The revenues of Limerick were not, as may well be supposed, very abundant. From his appointment to the see until 1755 he held the parishes of Newcastle and Monaghea, but in the May of 1755 he received power from Rome to take the parish of St. John's, vacated by the death of Dr. Leahy. It is likely he did not himself apply for this charge, for the Roman documents were transmitted through Dr. William

O'Meara, Bishop of Killaloe, whose delegate, James White, gave full possession to Dr. Lacy on the 3rd of July. And when he did accept St. John's, he retained only half the emoluments for his own use, and gave up the government of the two former parishes altogether.

Dr. Lacy's health began to fail about the beginning of 1756. He endured a long-continued sickness with much patience. Though every hour was devoted to spiritual duties, he thought he could do more still for the service of God. The jubilee at the accession of Clement XIII. commenced in Limerick on the second Sunday after Easter, 29th April, 1759, and lasted for a fortnight. The pious prelate used every exertion to avail himself of that merciful dispensation to atone for past sins, and to impart its blessings to others. But the labour was too much for his exhausted frame. In a few days after he was attacked with jaundice, then with dropsy, which terminated fatally in a short time. Having governed the diocese of Limerick wisely for twenty-one and a-half years, he resigned his pure soul into the hands of God at a quarter-past four a.m., on Saturday, the 4th of August, 1759. The next day his body was removed to Ardagh, and there buried, according to his own request, in the family tomb. A tombstone was placed over his grave by the Right Rev. Dr. Young, with this inscription:

"Beneath this stone are deposited the mortal remains of the Right Rev. Robert Lacy, who was R. C. B. of Limerick twenty-one and a-half years. He departed this life August 4th, 1759. R.I.P."

DANIEL KEARNEY, *suc.* 1760; *ob.* 1778.

Daniel Kearney, a native of Limerick city, received his collegiate education in Paris. In his academical studies he was highly distinguished, and took out with applause in the University of Sorbonne, then the most famous school on the continent, his degree of Doctor of Divinity. On his return to Ireland, about the year 1744, he brought with him excellent testimonials for conduct and literary acquirements. The best proof of his merit is, that though then quite a young man, he was chosen by the Most Rev. C. Butler as one of his delegates to decide the important controversy, to which we have already referred, between Dean Creagh on the one side, and the Revv. Messrs. M'Mahon and White on the other.

On the death of Dr. John Leahy in 1754, Dr. Kearney was appointed V.G. of Limerick. He took a leading part afterwards in all the proceedings against the Rev. Patrick Scanlan, and acted as Dr. Butler's official when the final sentence was pronounced on the 17th of June, 1757. He was parish priest of the united parishes of St. Patrick, Dereghalavin, and Kilmurry for many years before Dr. Lacy's death. I think he must have been appointed in 1745, because the leaf containing the records of that year is torn out of White's MS., and on that leaf I suppose was recorded the death of William Murphy, the former P.P., as well as the appointment of Dr. Kearney, neither fact being noticed anywhere else. White is extremely exact in details, and rarely, indeed, passes entirely over such events.

On the very day that Dr. Lacy breathed his last, the Rev. Dr. John Creagh, Dean of Limerick, summoned the canons and pastors of the diocese to meet in St. John's chapel, near the gates of the city, on the following Wednesday (August 8, 1759), at 11 a.m., for the election of a vicar-capitular. The canons attended, and the pastors, except three who were sick, and the Rev. Timothy Hayes, of Kilfinnan, who appointed in his stead the Rev. John O'Brien, of Kilmallock. It was debated for some time whether the right of election did not belong exclusively to the canons, seven of whom were present. It was, however, agreed, lest the archbishop should annul the election, that according to the tenor of the letter of Benedict XIV. in 1755, all the canons and parish priests should register their votes. The result was, what it would have been had the canons only voted, the unanimous election of Dr. Creagh as Vicar Capitular.

The following is the deed of election, which was soon after confirmed by Dr. James Butler, Archbishop of Cashel :—

"Cum per obitum Illusmi. ac Revmi. Domi. D. Rob. Lacy, ultimi epi. Limcis. 4ta die presentis Augusti, tenore litterarum apostolicarum SS. Patris Benedicti Papae XIV. datarum Romae apud S. Mariam Majorem sub annulo piscatoris die 8 Aug. an. 1755, omnis potestas eligendi Vic^m· Capitularem ad nos infra scriptos pertinet et spectat; quapropter omnes simul convenimus in capella parochiali S. Joannis Baptistae hac 8va die Aug. ad eligendum Vic^m· Capitularem juxta tenorem praedictarum litterarum apostolicarum, quod post invocationem S. Spiritus, rite et canonice peregimus, et Dominum Joanem Creagh, Doctorem et Decanum Ecclesiae Cathedralis Limericensis, in Vicarium Capitularem elegimus. Datum Limerici hac die 8va Aug. anno 1759".

Then follow the subscriptions of the chancellor, five prebends (the dean did not sign), and thirty priests. Appended was this certificate :—

"Nos infra scripti Protonotarii ac Notarii Apostolici per praesentes fidem facimus ac testamur nos praesentes fuisse cum supra scripti Domini Canonici, Doctores, ac parochi dioecesis Limericensis regulariter ad scrutinium processerunt, quorum omnes *una voce* Dom. Joan. Creagh in Vic. Capitularem elegerunt, omnesque suprascripti proprias manus affixerunt. In cujus rei fidem sigilla officii et manus proprias apponimus. Datum Limerici hac nona die Aug. 1759.

JOANNES DE LACY, S.T.D., Protonot. Apostolicus.
JACOBUS WHITE, Notarius Apost.
EDWARDUS O'BRIEN, Notar. Apost."

The next day after the election of the vicar, the same assembly of canons and pastors proceeded by scrutiny to the nomination of a bishop, and they chose Dean Creagh in the first place, David Bourke, P.P. of Rathkeale and Chancellor, in the second, and in the third Dr. Rowland Kirby, P.P. of St. Munchin's. We have but few, if any, printed forms of the deed of postulation as used in Ireland at that period. It may be then interesting to quote the document approved on this occasion, when, as far as I know, for the first time all the pastors in a diocese postulated for a bishop.

"Cum per obitum Illusmi. ac Revmi. Domi. Rob. Lacy Episcopi Limericensis quarta die praesentis mensis Augusti, sedes Episcopalis Limericensis vacaverit, Dominus Joannes Creagh, alias Creveus, Sacrae Theologiae Doctor, necnon Decanus hujus Ecclesiae Cathedralis canonicos in capitulum convocavit una cum Doctoribus ac parochis totius dioeceseos in ecclesia sancti Joannis Baptistae 4ta die infra octavam a die obitus, die scilicet 8va Augi.; ac dicta Missa de Spiritu Sancto, et omnibus servatis juxta consuetudinem ad electionem Vic. Capitularis per scrutinium processimus juxta tenorem litterarum Apostolicarum SS. Papae Benedicti XIV. datarum Romae apud S. Mariam Majorem sub annulo piscatoris die 8va Aug. an. 1755, ac una voce elegimus praelaudatum Dom. Joan. Craeveum in Vic. Capit. Et cum nihil nobis desiderabilius quam virum probitate, scientia, ac prudentia insignitum, qui nobis praecesset benignissime concedi, idcirco iterum convenimus ibidem hac nona die praedicti mensis, ac invocato Spiritu Sancto, ad scrutinium processimus, ac in primo loco elegimus unanimiter Dom. Joannem Creagh, alias Crevaeum (quem pridie in Vic. Cap. constituimus) nunc in Episcopum Limericensem; in secundo loco elegimus Dom. David Bourk, Cancellarium Ecclesiae Cathedralis in Epis. Lim.; in 3tio loco elegimus Dom. Rowlandum Kirby, Doctorem Theologiae in Ep. Lim.; Quapropter quam humillime petimus ac postulamus ut Sancta Sedes Apca. gratiose dignetur unum ex praedictis electis nobis concedere in Epis. Lim.; quoque et parochiam S. Joannis Baptistae, cum suis annexis (per obitum Illmi. ac Revmi. Episcopi R. Lacy nunc in curia vacantem) nemini, sede hac vacante conferre, utpote omnino necessariam ad episcopalem dignitatem sustinendam. Datum Limerici hac die 9na Aug. A.D. 1759".

To this document are subscribed the names of five canons and thirty other priests, among whom were a proxy and two administrators: none of the elect put their signatures. Then follows the certificate of the notaries apostolic in the same form as above, dated 9th of August, 1759. Nothing was likely to have a better effect than the unanimity of the clergy. Their postulation was indeed open to some objection, but it could not be called informal, and yet it utterly failed. Perhaps the right, which the clergy seemed to claim, and the strong form they used—*naming, electing, etc.*—gave offence in Rome, but the project did not fail for any defective form. The Roman authorities do not insist so rigidly on minutiae, as to exclude the best and fittest persons from high positions in the Church—because of some defect of mere form. The true cause of failure is more easily traced. While the clergy of Limerick were soliciting the promotion of their new Vicar Capitular, the Archbishop of Cashel, three of his suffragans, and some, it was said, of the clergy of Limerick, specially Dr. Conway, afterwards bishop, strongly recommended Dr. Daniel Kearney, and influenced chiefly by this recommendation, Pope Clement XII. appointed him Bishop of Limerick on the 21st of November, 1759. His bulls were expedited on the 27th of that month, and he was consecrated at Thurles, on the 27th January, 1760, by the Most Rev. James Butler, Archbishop of Cashel, assisted, not by bishops, but two priests, by special indult.

On the 31st of January, 1760, being the Thursday after his consecration, Dr. Kearney convened the clergy in the chapel of St. Mary's, Limerick, notified to them his election and consecration, and took formal possession of his see. He produced also a Bull collating on him the parish of St. John, with all its annexes, of which he took formal possession on Saturday, the 10th of May, 1760. He was inducted by the Rev. Michael Hoare, ex-provincial of the Dominicans, delegated for that purpose by the Archbishop of Cashel. The parish of St. Patrick's, hitherto held by Dr. Kearney, becoming vacant *in curia*, was conferred in January, 1761, by the Pope, on Rev. Denis Conway, who afterwards became Bishop of Limerick.

The Rev. James White, from whose MS. history we have taken these particulars, almost in his own words, has not recorded much to admire in Dr. Kearney's administration, or to justify the splendid hopes entertained by his friends at his first appointment. He admits, perhaps grudgingly, that the bishop's life was exemplary, and even austere; that he was easy of access even to the poorest of his people, and kind and affable to his clergy; but then he notices some official acts which nothing could justify but extreme necessity and the grant of extraordinary faculties from Rome, which, as far as I know, were not given to any other Irish bishop then or since. It may be that White, who betrays strong feeling now and again, was prejudiced against the successful rival of his friend, Dean Creagh, or that the bishop's mind was weakened by age and infirmity or the opposition of a disappointed clergy. Whatever be the cause, Dr. Kearney's ordinations, as described circumstantially by White, were certainly uncanonical, against the universal law of the Church (Trent, sess. xxiii. chap. 13), and the usage of this country, even in the worst of times. I know not a single precedent in our ecclesiastical annals since the Reformation for some of Dr. Kearney's practices in the collation of holy orders. The faculties should be very explicit, indeed, to justify such a manifest deviation from Church law; and if they had been granted, White must have heard of the concession. But if we except the manner of conferring orders, which cannot be defended, there is little else to blame in Dr. Kearney's conduct as a priest and bishop. His administration was marked by prudence and mildness, and, when duty required it, by apostolical firmness.

On Sunday, November 1, 1761, he publicly excommunicated from all the altars of the city a Dominican friar and a suspended secular priest, who had made themselves notorious for celebrating clandestine marriages, and he renewed a sentence of excommunication against a layman who assumed the character of priest to gain a living by celebrating such marriages. The trade of couple-beggar was a thriving one in many districts in those days, before the publication of the wise law of Trent forbidding clandestine marriages.

When the parish of Rathkeale became vacant in 1762, the Rev. William Nelan, a priest having few claims to promotion, left no means untried to obtain it. For this purpose he made every effort by personal application, the signatures of an immense number of the parishioners, and the earnest solicitations of Protestant gentlemen, who thought themselves entitled not to request, but to command, the bishop. His ambition and intrigues proved him eminently unfit for the position, and indeed for the sacred ministry. The bishop, therefore, on the 17th July, 1762, forbade the said Nelan from exercising any ecclesiastical function within that parish, and threatened suspension in case of disobedience. The parish was given in August to Rev. Laurence Nihell, afterwards Bishop of Kilfenora.

This same year, 1762, a proclamation was issued by Lord Halifax for a general fast and prayers. Copies of the form to be used were sent from the Castle to the Very Rev. Dr. Fitzsimons, V.G. of Dublin, with orders to transmit them to all the bishops, and to have the proclamation read publicly by the priests in their several chapels. Some of the bishops hesitated to use a public prayer sanctioned only by the Castle authorities. On the other hand, any resistance, however just or necessary, to the Government at that particular time, when the Whiteboys were disturbing the peace of the country, might be taken as an approval of their lawless course. The Dublin clergy substituted for the form in the proclamation another prayer to the same effect, which was read in all the churches on Quinquagesima Sunday, February 21, 1762. Dr. Kearney directed that though the priests should read the printed Government prayer (which was in form like a bishop's pastoral), they should omit the words, " I do earnestly exhort you to observe it exactly according to the tenor of the proclamation for that purpose", and to substitute, " The orders of our spiritual superiors are, that you exactly observe the same fast, and that you offer", etc., thereby precluding the notion that the State could of its own authority prescribe or modify the rites and ordinances and prayers of the true Church. Still it was too great a concession to accept in any shape a prayer drawn up by those without the Church, and more than one bishop refused even to appoint the same day for supplication that was fixed by the State.

Of the trouble caused by the Levellers and Whiteboys throughout the whole south, we have given a brief and authentic account in vol. i., p. 321. We shall add here the result of the Commission in Limerick, as described by White, who was present during the sittings of the court:

" On the 31st of May, a Commission of Oyer and Terminer was opened in Limerick. The judges were Lord Chief Justice Aston, an Englishman, and Judge Malone. They tried all the Levellers in Limerick Gaol, and, on the whole, it was found that a set of Protestant young fellows, who were intent on lowering the rent of lands, forced and compelled by firearms the poor people in their dependence to get out of their beds and to dig whatever lands they pointed out to them, to *level* walls, and some of them to kill cattle, the said Protestant fellows being always at their head. One Joseph Prestage, a Protestant, and one of the chief ringleaders, became King's evidence, and swore hard against the very poor creatures, whom, as he himself acknowledged, he forcibly compelled to do these mischiefs, and whom he furnished with arms for that purpose; one Banniard, a Protestant, and a chief of the party, and one Carthy, were sentenced to die for their killing of cattle. Five or six more of them were condemned to a year's imprisonment and some small fines. One William Trant, also a Protestant, one of the chiefs and the first-beginners of these troubles, was condemned to two years' imprisonment and a fine of £50. One Ley, also a Protestant, and a chief, was, through interest, received to be a King's evidence, in order to save his life; but I think he is also to be fined and confined. The rest of these Levellers the judges ordered to be discharged, without even paying any fees, as the judges considered them to be compelled to commit these irregularities by their Protestant leaders. The Protestants named above were men of property and consequence; and many more of them, against whom there are informations, have fled the country until the storm is blown over. No Catholic worth forty shillings was concerned in these riots, yet it was impudently reported, and even suggested to the Government, that it was the commencement of a Popish rebellion, and that the Papists were to massacre all the Protestants. But it happens now, that Protestants are justly condemned to die for what they would make out to be a Popish rebellion".

The commission appears to have checked and nearly eradicated the Whiteboy combination. While it lasted all the bishops of the south, but in a special manner the Archbishop of Cashel and the Bishop of Limerick, were kept in continual alarm. To the exertions made by both might be justly ascribed the suppression of a well organised conspiracy, which disregarded all right, public and private, and all law, civil and ecclesiastical. The latest fact recorded in connection with Dr. Kearney by Mr. J. White (deceased February 7th, 1768) is, that one Hurley, "a crack-brained" man, who had been ordained for the diocese of Emly by the Most Rev. J. Butler, endeavoured forcibly to fix himself in Limerick in the year 1767. His plea was, that he had been born in the diocese (whither his parents had removed for about a year), and recognized as a subject by Dr. Kearney in a letter to Paris, giving faculties for absolving him from any censures he may have incurred by being ordained in another diocese. When Hurley was challenged to produce the letter, it ran thus :

"Hurley, a secular priest of the diocese of Emly, may be absolved from any censures he might have incurred in the diocese of Limerick".

After reading the letter, Dr. Kearney immediately ordered him out of his apartments, and commanded him never again to return on the same errand. The unhappy man soon after abandoned the faith, turned parson, and died an apostate. With this sad story the Rev. James White closes his interesting annals, from which we have derived nearly all the facts of Dr. Kearney's life. From other sources we must form an estimate of his character, because White appears not to have appreciated it fully or honestly. The bishop's virtues were not likely to be understood by one who seems to have made up his mind from the very beginning not to be satisfied with his administration—to see nothing but faults. Prudence and discretion, a mild but inflexible firmness, were the most striking traits in his character ; he preferred the secure merit of governing quietly and unostentatiously to the glory which he might gain by novel and successful experiments. We have already called attention to the only practice —his system of conferring orders—which White justly condemns, and which, as far as we can see, cannot be excused or palliated. As a student he acquired in college a high reputation for talent and learning ; as a priest he obtained the highest and most confidential position that his discerning superiors could confer, and the esteem of successive archbishops of Cashel ; and, as a bishop, he was betrayed into few acts which his enemies could censure or pervert. He was vigilant in the discharge of his sacred office, and blameless in his private life. I have explained my views elsewhere (vol. i. p. 328) of the decrees of the Cork Synod, July 15, 1775, at which Dr. Kearney assisted, and of the ill-advised condemnation of the *Hibernia Dominicana* by him and his colleagues in the south, at Thurles, the same year. We will not, however, judge too severely the conduct of the prelates who take a share in these proceedings, if we give them credit for good motives, and doing what they thought best at a period of the most critical difficulty. It ought to be remembered, too, that Dr. Kearney was at the time of these councils weak in mind and body, and his labours nearly at an end. He resigned his soul into the hands of his Maker in the year of our Lord 1778, on the 24th of January.* The immediate cause of his death I have not yet discovered. His remains were interred in St. John's Churchyard, near the eastern wall, in the same tomb in which are deposited the bodies of the Very Rev. J. Leahy, V.G., his second predecessor in the parish of St. John's, and of the Rev. Owen O'Sullivan, Dr. Leahy's curate.—See Epitaph on tomb *infra* (end of Dr. Conway's life).

JOHN BUTLER, S.J., *appointed* 1778; *resigned*.

John Butler, son of Thomas, eighth Lord Cahir, by Frances, daughter of Sir Theobald Butler, was

* Mr. Lenihan (*History*, p. 627) writes : " His lordship died at *Ballyshannon, near Limerick*, in January, 1778".

appointed Bishop of Limerick on the 29th of March, 1778. On the 2nd February that year, Dr. Troy wrote to Dr. Butler, authorizing his Grace to use his name and signature in favour of the Honorable John Butler (vol. i., p. 350); and on April 4th the Archbishop of Cashel wrote to Father Butler, saying that the postulation in his favour " was backed by the signatures of three archbishops and twelve bishops of Ireland, by the Roman Catholic Peerage of Ireland, by the united letters of the Nuncios of Paris and Brussels, . . . and, to crown all, by the letters of your most worthy prelate, Dr. Walmesley". Father Butler first absolutely refused the honour, but, when pressed on all sides to give up his own will, he submitted, " on this condition, that if ever during my life the Society of Jesus be restored, I shall be at full and perfect liberty to re-enter the same, and retire again to my college, the seat of virtue and real happiness".

March 29, 1778, Secretary Borgia (ex-audientia) sends faculties to John Butler, Moderno Episcopo Limericensi, to promote six of his subjects to priesthood titulo Missionis, on condition of taking the usual oath. In the first week of July, 1778, the Bulls for his appointment were forwarded from Paris, and reached the Archbishop of Cashel about the 10th of the month. When his appointment was announced to the Jesuit father, he came over to Ireland, intending, we believe, to enter on his retreat before consecration. He visited, in the first place, his own family at Cahir, where he was waited on by some of the officials of the Diocese of Limerick. But he became more nervous than ever, and declared himself quite incapable of fulfilling the episcopal duties.

His firm resolution was now taken, he said, and nothing could prevail on him to accept such a fearful responsibility. In the following month Father Butler returned to Hereford [where he commenced his missionary labours on 4th April, 1760], to the great exultation of his numerous and very attached acquaintances.—See Dr. Oliver's *Collections*, p. 239, for a very interesting memoir of this saintly father. His connexion with Limerick ceased before September 8, 1778, on which day Cardinal Castelli wrote to the Archbishop of Cashel, requesting his Grace to send at once the formal renunciation of Limerick, and to give the brief to no one without orders from the Propaganda. This document shows very plainly that the Roman authorities were not, in the end, dissatisfied with Dr. Butler's resignation, dreading, perhaps, that he would not be well received by the clergy, many of whom petitioned for Dr. Nihell or Dr. Conway.

In our first volume, p. 356, are inserted two interesting letters from Dr. Troy, explaining the circumstances under which he signed the postulation for Dr. John Butler. The following letter to Dr. Carpenter regards the same subject, and explains fully the views of the Irish Bishops on the fasts prescribed by Government, to which reference has been made in Dr. Kearney's life :

"Kilkenny, 18th February, 1778.

"MOST HONOURED AND EVER DEAR SIR,—I desired Mr. O'Connor to inform you of the part I have acted relative to the present vacancy at Limerick, and flatter myself you are not displeased thereat, although you have recommended Mr. Nihell, against whom I have not the smallest objection, and for whom I would have subscribed very willingly if a letter from you or Dr. M'Mahon had reached me before my signature in favour of Mr. Butler, which I could not refuse for obvious reasons. I write to our worthy friend Charles Kelly this day, and send him a copy of Dr. Butler's letter to me, and of my answer on the occasion, in order he may be enabled to let Cardinal Castelli know how far I am interested in Mr. Butler's promotion. I think you would do well to write to Charles also about Mr. Nihell. The Cardinal and secretary have a great opinion of him, and I am sure he thinks himself happy in obliging you. In his last to me of the 31st December, he requested his most affectionate compliments to you, and desired me to acquaint you that the grant to England concerning the vigils of retrenched holidays would be extended to this entire kingdom. Your opinion on the propriety of publishing the approaching Government fast coincides with mine. Our neighbours of Munster deserve no compliment, and their example is no rule for me. Other circumstances, however, make me apprehend that my silence on the occasion would be misinterpreted, perhaps to the disadvantage of the clergy of this diocese in general. The spirit of Whiteboyism is not yet extinct in this county, and jurors and non-jurors equally wish for opportunities to show their abhorrence of every combination against Government. The latter are particularly desirous I should order an observance of the fast. Dr. Burke published the last one, and I find in his registry his exhortation on that occasion, which was repeated from every altar of the diocese, and also another similar one on the fast ordered by Government, March 10th, 1762. I am most sincerely inclined to act uniformly with my comprovincials, and particularly with you, my worthy Metropolitan, on all occasions. The above reasons and local circumstances seem to justify my deviation from that maxim on the present; wherefore, after mature deliberation and consultation, I have determined to notify the next fast without the sanction of your example, hoping you will not on that account doubt of my respect for your person, or suspect me of any uncanonical or unfriendly connexions with my extra-provincial neighbours, who, I assure you, are entirely ignorant of my aforesaid resolution. I am afraid Dr. Sweetman is not well. I wrote to him on the 20th ultimo, in answer to his letter, which I had the honour of showing you in Dublin, and, contrary to his custom, have not heard from him since. I hope you are free of your cold. "J. TROY.

"Dr. John Carpenter, Dublin".

DENIS CONWAY, *suc.* 1779; *ob.* 1796.

Denis Conway was born in the Diocese of Limerick, and at an early age was sent by his bishop, Dr. Lacy, to prepare for the sacred ministry in the University of Louvain. Having been ordained priest there, he returned to Ireland in September, 1757, and was immediately appointed parish priest of Glyn, vacant by the translation of Rev. T. Dundon to the parish of Nantinan (Stonehall). On the death of the Rev. Laurence Connell, one of the bishop's vicars (16th January, 1758), Dr. Lacy came with Mr. Conway on the 22nd January, and committed to him and the Rev. J. Creagh the care of the mensal parish of St. John's, allowing him one-fourth of the revenue for his support. The zeal with which he discharged his onerous duties in this new position won for him the respect of all the clergy of Limerick. On the promotion of Dr. O'Kearney to the episcopal dignity, the parish of St. Patrick's, held by him previously, became vacant in curia, and at the bishop's warm recommendation, who did not forget, it was thought, the zealous services of his friends during the vacancy, Dr. Conway was appointed parish priest by the Holy See. He obtained the bull to that effect in Jan. 1761, and officiated therein as pastor the following Easter. His great merits, indeed, appear to have gained for him the confidence of all his superiors, and there was no place of trust to which they did not raise him. Every where he displayed the same zeal and prudence that distinguished him afterwards as a bishop. He was subsequently promoted to the parish of St. Nicholas and vicarage of St. Mary's, when vacated by the death of the Rev. James White, the accomplished author of the *Annals of Limerick*. Here he continued till the year 1771, when, with the approval of the bishop, he exchanged with the Rev. Laurence Nihell, afterwards Bishop of Kilfenora, for the parish of Rathkeale, where this good priest laboured assiduously till the Almighty, through His vicar on earth, Pius VI., called him to rule the Diocese of Limerick in 1779. This appointment did not please the Archbishop of Cashel, who complained to Cardinal Castelli of the nomination without reference to himself. Dr. Moylan, too, was not consulted, and he thought the new bishop too delicate for active work :

"Tralee, May 2, 1779.

"MY EVER DEAR AND MOST HONOURED LORD,—The promotion of Dr. Conway to the See of Limerick I wish may answer the expectations of their Eminences. I fear the indispositions he is so much subject to will prevent the activity that the many wants of that diocese would require. He is much regarded by all the Protestant gentry, and I hope his conduct in the administration of his diocese will promote the spiritual welfare of his people. We have a very valuable acquisition in the new bishop of Meath. His talents, zeal, and politeness must render him an ornament to this poor National Church. Dr. Cahill writes to me that Dr. Plunkett is preparing to repair home. I think your Grace will find him a prelate according to your own heart. Poor Mr. Cahill is much indisposed with an obstruction in the liver; an excess of solicitude for the preservation of the community brought, in all appearance, that disorder on him. May God preserve him! I have the comfort of informing your Grace that my new chapel is advancing fast, the walls will be finished I expect in a fortnight, and I hope to have it roofed and slated by the middle of August. The plan I flatter myself will receive your approbation, when I have the honour and happiness of seeing you in these parts. I shall have a very fine sacristy and a spacious fine room over it for a library. The whole will be expensive, but I trust in God we shall be able to finish it in time. I presume the church at Thurles is nearly complete. I congratulate your Grace thereon. You will have a most comfortable chapel. May God, in His mercy to His people, grant you health and length of days to make use of it for His glory and the advancement of His holy religion.

"I have the honour of being, with sentiments of the most profound respect and the most cordial attachment, my ever dear and most honoured Lord, your truly affectionate and most devoted servant,

"F. MOYLAN".

A note added to Dr. White's MSS. in Dr. Conway's own handwriting, state that he was consecrated in July, 1779; but Dr. Young has supplied this correction:

"N.B.—Dr. Conway, whose handwriting this is, must have forgotten the date of his consecration, it having taken place on the 20th June, 1779, not in July; he died on Sunday morning, 19th June, 1796".

I have not been able to find in my collection of Bishops' letters many from Dr. Conway, though his name occurs often in the correspondence of others. The following is a summary of the most interesting documents in my hands:—

4th May, 1778.—Dr. Conway, *Vic.-Cap.*, writes from Adare to Rev. Mr. Young: "I don't doubt but the Hon. John Butler is appointed bishop; but neither could the archbishop nor he recall my powers, nor vest them in another, until he produces his letters of confirmation to the chapter or its representative, nor can he until then exercise any kind of jurisdiction in the diocese: see *Const.* of Boniface VIII., *Extrav. de Electione*, to which, Van Espen says, modern practice is conformable".

20th May, 1778.—Same to same: "Mr. Kelly's letter from Rome says, "The protest came too late, and therefore was suppressed. It is a wonder that Dr. Butler is not yet arrived. I expect every day to be summoned to town. Dr. Nihell will be naturally disappointed. I never set my heart on the issue of doubtful events".

The protest spoken of here against Dr. Butler, was forwarded about the 1st March, 1778, and signed by twenty-two parish priests. It was informal, however, because the Notary-Apostolic, the Rev. Mr. Walsh, prudently declined to affix his signature. The recommendation of the clergy in favour of Dr. Nihell or Dr. Conway, would, he said, have more weight in Rome, if sent forward by itself, without the strong protest against Dr. Butler. Dr. Nihell was supported by Dr. Carpenter, of Dublin, and by many of the clergy, including Dr. Conway himself.

17th June, 1778.—Dr. Conway tells Dr. Young, that yesterday se'nnight he received his letter, and next day set out for Cahir, where he was treated most kindly by the future bishop; praises his affability, knowledge of church discipline; heard it whispered that he was still disposed to decline; praises Lord Cahir and his princely style. Went also to Cashel, where he was graciously received by the archbishop; spoke to him about the protest of the clergy, excused them, when his Grace promised not to think of the matter any more.

12th August, 1778.—Same to Same: "Went to Tralee to see the kingdom of Kerry; got a cold in that wild district, which brought on my old physician the gout; both legs affected now so as not to be able to walk a step. I am told our bishop is to be in Limerick this week, and I regret very much I cannot be the first to pay him my respects". Asks Dr. Young to let him know the moment when the bishop comes, that he may cease to exercise capitular jurisdiction, and may send an apology. Dr. Young must also excuse him, and explain his absence.

26th August, 1778.—Same to same: "Has been in bed since 12th, but now just able to rise. Our bishop (Dr. Butler) acts, indeed, an odd part with regard to this diocese. He and his friends should have agreed on terms before matters were carried to such a length. This diocese is under no obligation to the archbishop. If Dr. Butler resigns, I am almost sure the Sacred Congregation will pay some some attention to the postulation of the clergy".

18th January, 1779.—" Abbé Fitzgerald, of Rome, writes to me that nothing will be done there till Dr. Butler's resignation is received, and that I would do well to send a fresh postulation. I have drawn out a short one in favour of Dr. Nihell, and got it signed by a good many. Others will sign it next Thursday, when the clergy of these decanates are to meet here to celebrate the anniversary of Dr. Kearney". Dr. Young prevailed on Dr. Conway not to forward this postulation. " I put him off of getting this postulation signed by the clergy of the eastern deanery, and it appears from what happened afterwards that I was right. J. Y."

8th February, 1779.—Rev. John M'Namara, parish priest Upperchurch (Cashel), informs Rev. Mr. Young that he heard this day from the archbishop, that Mr. Molloy, parish priest, Kilkenny, was elected to Limerick. [This rumour was unfounded.]

19th February, 1779.—Dr. Conway, in a letter to Dr. Young, expresses great surprise that the Sacred Congregation should thus disregard the recommendation of the clergy of this diocese and bishops of the province; the archbishop was, however, chiefly to blame. As to Dr. Young's proposed visit to Dr. Molloy, at Kilkenny, he had nothing to say; could not himself undertake the journey; requests Dr. Young to give enclosed letter to the bishop-elect, should he visit him at Kilkenny; if not send it by post. The result does not disappoint Dr. Conway, for he never is too confident when future contingencies are in question; is always prepared for either issue.

9th March, 1779.—The Rev. John M'Namara now announces Dr. Conway's election to Mr. Young.

10th March, 1779.—Dr. Conway thanks Dr. Young for all his kindness; must be ever grateful for his good opinion; grants permission to open the Nuncio's letter, or any other paper from abroad; for to Dr. Young, above and before all other men, would Dr. Conway make known all that interests himself.

1786, July 31st.—Dr. Conway wrote to the Archbishop of Cashel a strong denunciation of the Whiteboys, which I insert here as a fair specimen of his style, and a picture of his times:

"Limerick, July 31, 1786.

"MY EVER DEAR AND MOST HONOURED LORD,—Yesterday I was honoured with your Grace's letter, and am most heartily mortified at the distress your Grace is in on account of the diabolical and incorrigible conduct of the Whiteboys. Alas! what are all our labours, long journeys, and expenses turned to? What effect do our condescension and attention to their real or imaginary grievances produce? Nothing but rebellion against our jurisdiction, and an obstinate contempt of our zealous and salutary admonitions and instructions. I am in the same melancholy situation as your Grace. After my return from Cork I went to Newcastle, where I was immediately surrounded by hundreds of those deluded wretches in a tumultuous manner. I explained the regulations to them in Irish, and after speaking to them in the most feeling manner I could for better than two hours, the fruit I reaped was a declaration that they would to a man strictly observe the oaths they took; nay, they had the impudence to send me a copy of their resolution, which they expected I would sign. I got out among them, and declared that I was ready to suffer death rather than comply with their wishes; at the same time assuring them that my priests should lay no unnecessary burden on them. Upon this they seemed to be so well satisfied that they took the horses from my carriage and drew me amidst a thousand acclamations to this side of the turnpike. The better sort were highly pleased with the happy issue the clamorous business of the day had; but I was so far from being pleased, that I looked upon it as nothing else than the hosanna of a fickle mob. I therefore gave up the idea of making a visitation until they come to their reason. They are so convinced of the justice and lawfulness of their proceedings, that they hesitate not at calling for sacraments, and threaten that if refused they will shut up the chapels; but let the consequence be what it may, I never will admit one of them until he makes an entire submission. The infection is spreading through Dr. M'Mahon's diocese so rapidly, that when he visited Castleconnell parish they all walked out of the chapel, and would not listen to one word from him.

"Thus your Grace sees how near we are to a total overthrow of religion in this province, if the Almighty does not soon stretch forth His hand to avert it.

"I am very glad to hear that the College of Salamanca is again open to receive our subjects, though the prospect they have before them is discouraging enough. I mean to send one there this season. I desired to send me 20 sets of Appleton's Sermons, though I now doubt whether our priests will be able to purchase them, as they do not receive enough to support themselves, even in the most frugal manner. The Masses celebrated on the 25th of March *pro intentione piae personae* amount to the number of 58, my own included. As soon as I can learn where to address to Dr. Nihell, I will impart the contents of your Grace's letter to him. My little family present their most dutiful address to your Grace. My bodily health (thank God) is pretty well, though I am sick in mind; but whilst I live, I never will cease to be, my ever dear and honoured Lord, your Grace's most affectionate, devoted, and humble servant,

"DENIS CONWAY.

" To the Archbishop of Cashel".

1793, March 4th.—Same to same, on policy of Catholics; cannot explain why Dr. Young's Bulls have not arrived, because he had a letter dated 5th December, from his Roman agent, announcing the appointment; his own health much weakened by labour and anxiety.

1793, April 20th.—Asks Dr. Bray to fix a day for Dr. Young's consecration, whose Bulls come to hand on the 18th instant.

Dr. Conway departed this life on the 19th day of June, 1796, and was buried in the same grave with Dr. Kearney, in the churchyard of the Protestant Church, called St. John's, Limerick.

The inscription on the horizontal slab over the grave of Drs. Kearney and Conway, Bishops of Limerick, runs thus:

"In this sepulchre are deposited the remains of the Right Rev. Denis Conway, Roman Catholic Bishop of Limerick, and parish priest of St. John's parish, in said city, who departed this life on the 19th day of June, 1796, in the 74th year of his age".

In this epitaph there is no reference whatever to

Dr. Kearney, though he was buried in the same grave. So in the epitaph on Dr. Young's monument, there is no allusion to Dr. Tuohy, who rests in the same tomb.

JOHN YOUNG, *cons.* 1793 ; *ob.* 1813.

Dr. John Young, Bishop of Limerick, was born of William Young and Mary Cahill, in St. John's Parish, and baptized 10th March, 1746.* He matriculated at Louvain in 1765, made his first printed thesis in 1770, and took his degree of A.M. on 11th October, same year. He was ordained sub-deacon, December, 1768; deacon, 23rd September, 1769; priest in 1770, and soon after (in July, 1771) sent on the mission to Ireland by the Nuncio Ghilini. After his return home, he served successively as curate of St. John's, parish priest of Bruff, parish priest of St. John's, and resided, in 1778-80, opposite John's Church, near John's Gate, in Irishtown, Limerick. From the very beginning of his labour, even as Catholic curate, he enjoyed the entire confidence of his bishop, who relied much on his aid and counsel. The earliest allusion to Dr. Young's name as the intended successor to Dr. Conway, is contained in the following letter from Dr. Butler's Roman agent, Valentine Bodkin. It is dated Rome, December 25, 1790, and addressed to his Grace of Cashel:

"Dr. Conway, of Limerick, has lately recommended Mr. Young for the deanery vacant by the death of the late Dean Creagh; he runs the highest encomiums on said Young, and is leaving no stone unturned to have him appointed his *coadjutor*. I am credibly informed said Mr. Young is not all he

* Born 21st April, according to Dr. Bray's return in *Roman Almanack*.

is represented by Dr. Conway. Seem to know nothing of this from me. Your Grace will and must be consulted by Rome on this occasion; therefore make yourself easy till you are consulted, when, I am sure, you will do what the interests of religion dictate, without yielding to blind feeling or affection. I have reason to believe that neither Dr. M'Mahon nor Dr. Conway would show you any attachment or deference more than what their being your suffragans and your being their metropolitan obliges them to. Therefore be more than on your guard in recommending any of their favourites, for they would readily make a stand against you. *Dr. Conway made use of Dr. O'Kelly here* in getting the Papal Bulls of the deanery for Dr. Young, although last year his reply to me was, 'he wanted no regular agent, but when occasion required would employ me'".

This last paragraph explains fully the opposition of Mr. Bodkin to Drs. Conway and Young, and his bitter enmity to Dr. Troy and all his friends who employed as their Roman agent the Rev. Charles O'Kelly, O.P.

I have observed elsewhere that the seeds of dissension between Dr. Butler and his supporters on the one side, and Drs. Carpenter and Troy on the other, were certainly sown by Roman agents. No one can read the letters of Bodkin or of his predecessor in the same office, the Rev. A. Cuccagni, without noticing the hostile spirit to Dr. Troy which animates the writers. Their wrath is provoked by the very name of Dominican, and every one connected with that Order is their enemy. Against their insinuations the reader must be constantly on his guard.

Shortly after Dr. Young's promotion to the deanery, he was appointed parish priest of St. Mary's. On Feb. 9, 1791, Mr. Bodkin wrote thus again to Dr. Butler:

"Your two letters (December 11 and January 12) came most seasonably, and saved both you and Dr. Conway, for I immediately spoke to Cardinal Antonelli, who, upon my remonstrating the purport of your letter, and the necessity of indulging Dr. Conway by conferring the parish on Mr. Young, as his lordship recommended, consented, after some difficulty; and, though Dr. Connolly, Dr. Conway's agent, handed in a petition two months before, it would not have been granted but for you: in the very rescript is inserted *attenta Archiepiscopi Cassiliensis*, etc. This rescript was forwarded to Dr. Conway on 29th January, by way of Liege, where the Nuncio now resides".

Dr. Young's election as coadjutor bishop was confirmed by the Pope on Sunday, December 2, 1792, though I find a different date (4th January, 1793) in Dr. Bray's return to Father Concannon for the *Roman Almanack*. Dr. Conway wrote to Dr. Bray, April 20, 1793, stating that the Bulls came to hand on the 18th instant, having been posted at Maestricht and sent through the Nuncio at Brussels. The letter closes with a request that his Grace would consecrate the new prelate, who will be an ornament to the Church. Dr. Young was consecrated bishop of *Maxula in partibus*, in St. Mary's Church, Limerick, May, 20, 1793, by Dr. Bray, assisted by Drs. M'Mahon and Egan (Waterford). At the ceremony were present also Drs. Conway, Teahan, and Coppinger.

I have seen several letters, some still in my hands, from Dr. Young to the archbishop and bishops of the province. In all of them may be traced the same pure and gentle spirit which marked the bishop's whole life. Worldly maxims, political strife, family relations, even the usual friendly compliments, never occupy his thoughts. He has but one idea, how to advance religion and to provide for the wants of the ministry. His only anxiety is to conform rigidly to the discipline of the Church, and to discharge his duties faithfully.

The following summary gives a fair notion of the subjects treated of in those letters, quoted in the order of time:—

1793, March 19.—Thanks Dr. Bray for letter of 13th inst., congratulating him on his appointment, and asks to be remembered in his prayers.

1796, June 19.—Announces with deep regret the death of Dr. Conway at an early hour this morning. He feels that he has lost his best friend in this world.

1798, December 28.—Dr. Young, in a letter dated "near Limerick", writes thus to Dr. Bray: "I think the government pension well intended, but it may destroy confidence of flock, create contentions, and open a door for government patronage, intrigue, and simony. On the whole, as far as I can see, I am against it, either for all or for any, even the needy; so is Dr. M'Mahon".

1798, December 31.—To the same: "A government proclamation has opened my eyes about the pension. I see now it is a *douceur to carry the Union*, and though not perhaps so decided against that measure as some of my colleagues, *I will never take a bribe to annihilate Ireland's independence*".

1799, April 22.—Wrote to Dr. Bray about the necessity of increasing number of students in Maynooth College; quite opposed to entrance fees and heavy expenses of any kind.

1800, November 5th.—Acknowledges receipt of Dr. Bray's letter of the 25th October, and adds: "I am confined this last month by erysipelas in the leg, which, though now abated, prevents me from going to Dublin. Dr. O'Shaughnessy has been similarly affected for some weeks, but has been out the last few days. He and Dr. M'Mahon have sent, I believe, their answers to Dr. Troy on the subject of your Grace's letters. *As for my part, I candidly acknowledge I never liked to become a pensioner to government, Timeo Danaos, etc.*, and am not without my fears of the consequences of the measure to the ecclesiastical body in this country, and the interest of religion; but I fear the die is cast, I am in a minority, and, of course, all opposition is fruitless and vain. What remains for me then is to wish and pray that my apprehensions may not be realized. There is no chapter in this diocese at present. My late predecessors let it die out to prevent rivalry among the clergy, and I have not renewed it for the same reason, so that there is no office attached to the deanery but that of assembling the parish priests when the see becomes vacant".

1804, July 3.—To the same, on Maynooth and the re-opening of Salamanca; regrets much to hear of Dr. Dillon's bad health at Bath, encloses copy of rescript authorizing him to take small offerings on the occasion of marriage dispensations, and refers to decree in *Hib. Dominicana*, p. 179, on same subject.

1807, March 21.—Calls Dr. Moylan's attention to the contents of a book published in Limerick, apparently with sanction of some friars, promising indulgences which he can hardly think authentic, such as indulgences of 28,000 years, and other almost endless periods. Sacred things should not be exposed to ridicule under the pretence of promoting piety.

1808, August 15.—To Dr. Bray. Warm protest against meeting of bishops, or opening again question of veto.

1808, November 9.—To Dr. Coppinger: " It is only the party in Dublin favourable to veto, and disappointed at our resolutions, that are propagating reports about meetings to censure them: but even so, they cannot gather a meeting; the least religious of my people are against this insidious measure. I am concerned that Dr. Troy should regret that any time-serving expressions were not prefixed to the word 'inexpedient'; it would be laying a snare for involving ourselves or posterity in the perplexing circumstances we have so happily escaped, *and I hope the question of the veto is now put down for ever, and I believe, from the unanimity with which it was carried, that the resolution against the veto was suggested by the Holy Ghost*". His own health not good for the last two years; just recovered from a severe attack of gout, which the doctors tell him was the cause of his sickness.

The meeting of the bishops alluded to by Dr. Young was held September 14, 1808, and the resolution adopted against the veto was this :

" It is the decided opinion of the Catholic prelates of Ireland here assembled, that it is INEXPEDIENT to introduce any alteration in the canonical mode hitherto observed in the nomination of Irish Catholic bishops, which mode long experience has proved to be unexceptionally wise and salutary".

Before the word *inexpedient*, Dr. Troy proposed to insert NOW or IN THE PRESENT CIRCUMSTANCES, but his suggestion was rejected.

1809, February 26.—To Dr. Bray. Dr. Young signs his name with a cross prefixed, the earliest I have seen: "Gave leave for meat one day more in this Lent, on account of unequalled scarcity of fish. The September resolution against the veto gives here immense and universal satisfaction. I think the answers of Drs. Coppinger and Power to Dr. Milner's Letter to a Parish Priest have beaten his Lordship out of the field of controversy; it is a comfort as well as a credit to the hierarchy of this country to have set aside the question of the veto for ever".

1810, January 17.—Acknowledges receipt of Dr. Bray's letter of the 12th instant, enclosing copies of Dr. Milner's letters of 16th December and 3rd January; cannot understand Dr. Milner's silence, and blames Dr. Moylan's; cannot accept any one of the three proposals of Dr. Milner; thinks Drs. Coppinger and Power the fittest representatives to be sent to London, and advises a joint letter to the Pope and another to his vicar against the veto; always dissented from, and now laments, the Maynooth resolution of 1799, which Dr. Milner, in his Letter to a Parish Priest, has taught our enemies to use.

1810, August 8.—States that the Catholic Committee are for local, immediate, and frequent meetings of the Catholics; doubts the expediency of this course, because the enemy will disturb the country, to throw odium on us. They always did so, and will play the same game again.

1810, November 21.—Consults archbishop on the nature of his faculties from Rome; does not understand the clause, "promovendi ad ordines sine limitatione", which he thought every bishop had in this country from usage or previous grant, nor that of dispensing in *mixed* marriages; complains of the short course of theology in Maynooth, and suggests two professors for Dunboyne students, one for Canon Law and History, the other for Dogmatic and Moral Theology, if many students should be placed on the foundation.

1810, December 13.—Writes to Dr. Moylan: "The zeal Mr. Mahony and his brother have for establishing a convent of the Presentation here has met with a disappointment which I trust will be only temporary. He will inform you himself of the progress of his exertions towards accomplishing the object, and he carries with him two letters I received from Mrs. M'Loughlin, the Reverend Mother of Kilkenny, by which your Lordship will see the obstacles yet to be surmounted. It is an old observation, that most establishments from which much good was to be expected had great difficulties to encounter in their commencement, but were gradually got over, and I trust the case will be the same here. Wishing your Lordship a full measure of the benedictions attending the approaching festivals, I have the honour to be,

"Your respectful and obedient servant,

"✠ JOHN YOUNG".

The good bishop could have hardly anticipated the difficulties that arose immediately after, in consequence of which the convent of the Presentation Order was not founded for more than a quarter of a century. The education of young females was not, however, neglected during Dr. Young's time. A school was opened for their benefit in Newgate Lane under the care of Miss Young, the bishop's sister, a pious and accomplished lady, whose name is still revered by the faithful people of Limerick.

1813, May 16.—In answer to Archbishop's (Cashel) notice of a general meeting of prelates in Dublin on the 25th, Dr. Young says he expected this meeting would be necessary ever since the letter of the English Board to ours, from which he concluded that Mr. Dillon and his associates had betrayed us by agreeing to some resolutions in the bill they gave to Castlereagh. Dr. Troy then thought a meeting not necessary or advisable. Our Board seems to have flinched from the sentiments they heretofore expressed of declining the acceptance of emancipation if the independence of their religion was to be sacrificed to it; now that a favourable prospect of emancipation appears in view, the interest of religion is thrown into the background that it should not be embarrassed, forsooth, by the discussion of polemics.

This letter, written but a few months before the bishop's death, is the last document of interest from him that we have seen.

" There was no diocesan seminary or college at that period in Munster, except the small one at St. Peter's cell, Limerick, and that of St. John's, Waterford, when Dr. Young conceived the idea of founding a college suited to the increasing requirements of the diocese. In this he was aided not only by the clergy, but by the Catholic citizens, who in 1805 had entered into large subscriptions for the purpose. The site was at Park, within the demesne of Park house, which Dr. Young had purchased for £1,800, as a residence for the bishops of the diocese. He presided over the college, which sent out many distinguished clergymen.

" The college existed until 1830, when the students were drafted to Waterford, Carlow, Maynooth, etc., but the building was not removed until 1864"—Mr. Lenihan's *History*, p. 422.

It was natural that Dr. Young, taking into account his own tastes and acquirements, should make great exertions to promote the cause of education. He was himself through life a close student and a profound scholar. He was passionately fond of mathematics, and even in his old age and declining health he devoted some time each day to his favourite study. But he did not neglect the knowledge which regards more immediately the duties of a priest and bishop. For the guidance of his clergy, he issued two or three editions of the diocesan statutes of Dr. Lacy with important changes. He insisted very strongly on punctual attendance at the ecclesiastical conferences, at which he always presided ; and he never ordained any of his subjects without a searching examination in Dogmatic and Moral Theology. For the instruction of children he published an excellent catechism in English and Irish, which is still in use throughout part of the diocese. Of Dr. Young's habits in private little has been recorded, but the few glimpses that we get of his domestic life show him to be a prelate of exalted virtue. He made it a rule never to sleep on a soft bed. When at home his only couch was the hard board. His food was of the plainest kind, abstaining altogether from flesh meat during Advent and Lent, and from strong drink at all seasons. He devoted much time to prayer, and distributed alms with his own hand to the sick poor. In simplicity of manners, singleness of purpose, piety, and self-denial, Dr. Young was "made a pattern of the flock from the heart".

There is an addition to White's MS. in Dr. Tuohy's handwriting, which I copy verbatim :

"John Young was coadjutor bishop at the time Dr. Conway died, in 1796. He was a learned, zealous, pious, prudent, retiring, but hospitable prelate, who lived beloved, and died regretted by his clergy, on the morning of the 23rd September, 1813, between the hours of twelve and one o'clock, and was succeeded by Charles Tuohy, consecrated April 23rd, 1815, in Cork".

At the close of the Lent before Dr. Young's last sickness, his strength seemed to be entirely exhausted by rigorous fasts. He went through the ceremonies of Holy Week with the greatest difficulty, and yet no importunity of friends or medical advisers could induce him to relax the rigours of his mortification. One day a good country parish priest bluntly told the bishop that he needed nothing but the use of more generous diet. But Dr. Young would not touch "the fat beef-steak" recommended by his good-natured visitor, reminding him of the apostle's saying: "If meat scandalize my brother, I will never eat flesh, lest I should scandalize my brother". "Good father", added the saintly old man, "my soul's health needs this mortification, and why should I in my old age, be so anxious about prolonging life for a few days?"

It is not often, unhappily, that much lustre is added to the life of an ecclesiastic by the virtues of his family. It is an old sad proverb: The nearer the Church, the farther from God. But the history of the Young family forms certainly a notable exception to the adage. Charles Young, one of the bishop's brothers, came up to Dublin at an early age, and began business in the firm of Young and Lynch, successors to Hevey and Co., Castle Street. The partners married two sisters, daughters of Mr. Hevey, their predecesor in trade. Mr. and Mrs. Young were blessed with a numerous family —eight sons and four daughters. Of the daughters three died nuns, one, Catherine (in religion Mary John), Mother Abbess of the Poor Clares, Harold's Cross, Dublin, two in the Ursuline Convent, Cork, the authors of the popular *Ursuline Manual*, a *History of England*, and other well known works. The fourth daughter died during her noviciate in a religious house. The history of their brothers is yet more remarkable: four became priests, of whom the youngest, Charles, born 21st December, 1798, is still living, a Jesuit Father in Clongowes Wood College; William, the eldest of the priests, at one time parish priest of Baldoyle and Howth (having for his curates his two brothers), died about 1855, during a mission in Middlesex, having preached the Gospel for a long time to the poor Irish in Liverpool, Gravesend, Bayswater, Hanwell, and Cornwall; James, the late parish priest of St. Margaret's, born 1796, died 18th September, 1862 ; and Henry, born June 7th, 1786, for many years chaplain to St. Joseph's Asylum, a man truly wise in good and simple in evil, who departed this life in the odour of sanctity, on the 17th of November, 1869. With the Revv. Fathers Henry and James Young the writer had the happiness of being long and intimately acquainted, and more perfect models of that ideal holiness, of which we read only in the lives of the saints, he never knew.*

In the badly enclosed churchyard, called St. Patrick's, Limerick, about half a mile outside the city on the south-east, Dr. Young is buried. A neat monument, enclosed with an iron paling, is over the grave with this inscription :

" This monument was erected at the expense of the parish clergymen of this diocese, to the memory of the Right Rev. John Young, who departed this life on the 22nd day of September, 1813, in the sixty-eighth year of his age, and twentieth of his episcopal dignity. His life was truly exemplary and apostolical; he was remarkable for his piety, charity, and profound learning: humble and mortified in his manner of life, he sought only the honour and glory of God, and not the things of this life; he died regretted by his clergymen, to whom he was a faithful instructor, and lamented by the poor, to whom he was a parent and protector. May his soul rest in peace. Amen".

* We are rejoiced to see that an accomplished and noble lady is now engaged in writing a beautiful Memoir of Father Henry Young for the *Irish Monthly*, a new magazine of great merit.

In the same grave are also the remains of Dr. Tuohy, who requested to be buried with his predecessor, for whom he entertained the greatest esteem and veneration. But there is no reference whatever to Dr. Tuohy in the epitaph, which was written by himself, to commemorate the virtuous life of his ever faithful and attached friend, Dr. Young.

CHARLES TUOHY, *cons.* 1815; *ob.* 1828.

Dr. Tuohy was a native of the city of Limerick, where he received his early classical education. He pursued his early ecclesiastical studies first and chiefly at Bordeaux, where he became acquainted with Dr. Everard, Archbishop of Cashel, and after at Toulouse and Paris. Having spent about eight years in preparing himself for the sacred ministry, he was ordained priest in 1780, and returned in the beginning of 1784 to Ireland, his first mission being St. John's, Limerick, where he was much esteemed as a preacher. He was appointed afterwards in succession parish priest of Newcastle, parish priest of Rathkeale, and dean of the diocese, and displayed in every position great zeal and piety. On the death of Dr. Young he was nominated vicar capitular in September, 1813, by the whole body of pastors in the diocese, who met at St Mary's, Limerick. Their resolution he himself made known to the Archbishop of Cashel, and recommended at the same time the Rev. P. Hogan, pastor of St. Michael's, as a worthy representative of the chapter. The clergy chose himself indeed, because he was more familiar with Dr. Young's views, as being for many years one of his lordship's council of seven priests. The archbishop did not hesitate to approve the choice of the clergy, and Dr. Tuohy acted accordingly as vicar capitular. When writing that letter to the archbishop he understood very well that the election as vicar capitular was but a step to a higher dignity, that it must bring him more prominently under the notice both of the priests of Limerick, who signified their intention of recommending him to the Holy See, and specially of the bishops of the province, many of whom were already favourably disposed in his regard. He therefore entreated the archbishop to approve of Father Hogan as vicar capitular, but in vain. His Grace and his suffragans were quite resolved to support no other candidate for the vacant see. Dr. O'Shaughnessy wrote two letters to the archbishop, recommending Dr. Tuohy strongly. In the first, 8th July, 1814, he requests Dr. Bray to support the postulation for Dr. Tuohy, as "the confidant, the dean, and the intended successor of Dr. Young"; and in the second, 21st July, 1814, he urges further, that Dr. Young made him dean and vicar-general with a view to succession, and that even the removal of Dr. Tuohy to Limerick since his appointment as vicar capitular would make it now inconvenient to have him set aside. Like commendations were addressed to the archbishop by the other Munster prelates, and their united suffrages had, no doubt, much influence in the final decision at Rome.

On 4th October, 1814, Father Connolly wrote to the archbishop from St. Clement's, stating that Drs Everard and Tuohy had been appointed bishops, and that the usual documents would be sent through Dr. Murray, Archbishop of Dublin. On the 25th of the same month Dr. Troy wrote to Dr. Bray, informing him that, from a letter of Dr. Murray's, dated Rome, 29th September, he could learn that Drs. Everard, Kelly,

Plunkett, Waldron, Marum, Murphy, and Tuohy were appointed (on 19th September, as I infer from other sources) respectively to Cashel (coadjutor), Tuam, Elphin, Kilkenny, Cork, and Limerick.

14th November, 1814, Dr. Tuohy, in a letter to Dr. Bray, says: Is told he is appointed bishop; afraid of the labour and responsibility after thirty years' hard mission; only just recovered from a severe bilious attack, being much served by the Castleconnell spa; rejoices to hear of Dr. Everard's promotion, with whom he was intimately acquainted formerly at Bourdeaux; hopes he will not decline; as for himself he is quite unable from health to bear the heavy burden, but will obey, trusting in Divine Providence.

March 1st, 1815.—Same to same. Drs. Plunkett and Waldron have been consecrated in Dublin; Drs. Troy and Murray go to Kilkenny this week to consecrate Dr. Marum; thence to Tuam to consecrate Dr. Kelly; fears, as Dr. Sughrue is unwell, and Dr. Archdeacon is unable to attend, there must be a long delay before his own consecration.

Many of the Irish sees had been vacant at this time in consequence of the disturbed state of the continent and the Pope's exile: For example, there was no appointment to Tuam from 1809 to 1814, none in Ossory from February, 1812, to end of 1814. The exile and imprisonment of the Pope prevented the free exercise of his authority. It was his first care after the restoration to provide for the vacant sees. This was the reason why so many Irish bishops were now appointed together, and why it was so difficult to consecrate them in their respective cathedrals. It was no easy matter in those days to make a journey from Dublin to Kilkenny and thence to Tuam, thence again to Limerick, and many of the prelates were aged, and infirm, and poor.

Hence Dr. Tuohy found it more convenient to proceed to Cork, where he and Drs. Everard and

Murphy were consecrated by Dr. Coppinger on 23rd April, 1815. On his return to Limerick he applied himself at once to the zealous discharge of his duties, and displayed more energy in visiting the several parishes, preaching the word of God, etc., than could be expected from one habitually so delicate. During his administration of the diocese, he won the esteem of his own flock by his meek and gentle disposition, and the respect of those who differed from him in religious belief by his graceful manners and blameless life.

Dr. Tuohy took an active part against the veto. While vicar-capitular it became his duty to lead the clergy of Limerick in opposing that measure. Quarantotti's famous rescript was despatched from Rome on the 16th of February, 1814. It was directed to Dr. Troy, who sent copies to the other archbishops, with a short decisive letter to this effect :

My dear Lord,

"Rescripta Roma venerunt, causa finita est. By the enclosed copy your Grace will perceive that the *veto* has been granted by the Holy See to his Majesty our Sovereign. Whatever be our sentiments on the subject, it is our duty to acquiesce in the decision of such authority, and set the example of submission to it. Please, my Lord, to send copies of the enclosed to your suffragan prelates, and believe me, with great respect and haste,

"Your Grace's devoted and humble servant in Christ,

"J. T. Troy".

The vast majority of the bishops decided at once that *Rome had not spoken*, and that the rescript had no binding force. The Primate said, "That if the Pope even ordered him to consecrate a bishop, appointed according to the veto arrangement, for any diocese, that he would remonstrate, and rather than comply resign his crozier". The Archbishop of Cashel held that the question had been already settled by the Holy See in 1805, citing the words of Benedict XIV. to the Bishop of Breslau :

"In ecclesiastical history there is not recorded a single example of allowing the appointment of a Catholic bishop to a sovereign of another religion; he would not and could not introduce an example that would scandalize the whole Catholic world; for besides the dreadful judgment inflicted on him in the next world, he would render his name odious and accursed during life, and more so after death".

Archbishop Murray, coadjutor of Dublin, compared the misguided Catholics who were willing to impose new and disgraceful bonds on Christ's mystic body, to the Jews who bound Him to a pillar.

Dr. Power refused to go to any meeting of the bishops to reconsider the question :

"The veto is settled, specially as the laity has joined us: our meeting would indicate a wavering, and make them waver. And we must not yield to any resolutions of the English Catholics. After all, the English Catholics are to take the lead. They ever had it in surrendering their religion; we, I hope, shall not now begin to follow them".

Dr. O'Shaughnessy would have nothing to do with any further meeting :

"I have nothing to do there: the question is already disposed of: we are pledged to each other and the public. What then should we meet about? Let Dr. Troy put this notion out of his head. May the hand be paralysed that will ever sign for a veto in any shape or form".

Dr. Coppinger would not heed Dr. Troy's application to meet:

"I will not go; if you go, your Grace (Cashel) is hereby empowered to sign for me against the fifth resolution of the English Catholics, and against every modification of the infamous veto".

The priests were still more determined than the bishops. They held meetings in almost every diocese, and denounced all interference direct or indirect of the Crown in the nomination to Irish sees. Thirty-six parish priests of the diocese of Limerick met at St. Michael's church on the 28th of May, 1814, and unanimously resolved:

" First—That the rescript, signed B. Quarantotti, should not be obeyed by the Catholic Church; secondly—that they would hold no communication whatever with Monsignor Quarantotti or Dr. Poynter on this unauthorized document; thirdly—that they felt themselves called upon particularly to defend the sacred deposit of faith, because their brave ancestors, while defending their civil rights within the walls of Limerick, obtained the guarantee of a solemn treaty for the free and full exercise of the ancient religion of Ireland.

"Signed, CHARLES TUOHY,
" Vic.-Cap. of the Diocese of Limerick, and thirty-five other parish priests".

See "A Letter to the Roman Catholic Priests", by C. O. (Conroy of Ossory).

Among the most useful enterprises sanctioned by Dr. Tuohy during his administration may be mentioned the establishment of the Christian Brothers' Schools in Sexton Street and Clare Street, in June, 1816. The time was ill suited for religious reforms, when the Catholics were devoting all their energy to the great struggle for civil rights, which continued until the bishop's death.

1825, May 26 —Dr. Tuohy informed Dr. Laffan that Rev. Mr. Hanigan, his Roman agent, states that Rev. Mr. O'Finan peremptorily refuses to be appointed his coadjutor; does not believe it, but thinks he was objected to from Ireland; blames the agent as uncandid; will not write to him again; wrote this day to Rome, saying that he now thinks Dr. O'Finan's appointment would not be acceptable to the prelates of the south. He is inexperienced in Irish missionary work, and perhaps not pleasing to the British Government because of his long residence in Rome. He therefore urgently pressed the authorities of Propaganda to appoint the Rev. John Ryan, referring them to his Grace for Mr. Ryan's character. Dr. Laffan will, no doubt, bear witness to Mr. Ryan's merits.

1825, October 22.—Same to same: Received yesterday a letter from Rome, dated October 1st, stating that Propaganda met on 19th September, and on 25th decreed to appoint Rev. John Ryan coadjutor of Limerick. The Pope confirmed the election the same day. The Bull has been already despatched, and may be expected to arrive very soon. Dr. Tuohy rose from his bed of sickness, suffering from hemorrides, to write this joyful news, so agreeable to himself and to his Grace.

I find no letters of later date written by Dr. Tuohy. His character and virtues are thus described by the Protestant editor of a local journal in its obituary:—

"The episcopal dignity was perfectly unsolicited by Dr. Tuohy, for his habits were naturally of a modest and unassuming tendency; yet, when occasion required it, he exercised its important functions with vigour and determination. In the years 1819, 1820, and 1821, when the county felt violently agitated by insurrectionary movements, the pastoral letters of Dr. Tuohy, denouncing the evil spirit which stalked abroad, and enjoining loyalty to the crown and obedience to the constituted authorities, circulated throughout the diocese, and were echoed from the altar and the pulpit, and acknowledged to have had a happy effect in checking the atrocities of a deluded peasantry. On a subsequent occasion, Dr. Tuohy was equally energetic in repelling an unjustifiable attack on the character of his Church and her clergy. Eventually his health declined, and since December, 1825, he gave up the management of an extensive diocese to Dr. Ryan, his coadjutor, who is now Roman Catholic Bishop of Limerick, his worthy predecessor having fallen into the grave full of years and honours"—Obituary notice in *Limerick Chronicle.*

Dr. Tuohy departed this life on Monday evening, 18th March, 1828, at his residence, Newtown ville, near Limerick, at the advanced age of seventy-four, having nearly completed the 14th year of his episcopacy.

On the morning after his decease, the remains were brought to St. John's chapel, and the offices of the Church were recited constantly until the burial on Wednesday, the 19th. The funeral procession was the most imposing seen for many years in the city of Limerick. The mayor attended in his robes of office, the sheriff of the county and his under sheriff, the Protestant dean and archdeacon, a vast assemblage, without distinction of class or creed, all vying with one another to testify their regret for the honoured dead About two o'clock, after the solemn office and Mass, the procession moved on from St. John's, by the Square, Broad Street, etc., to the churchyard of St. Patrick's, where the body was deposited in the tomb raised to the memory of the venerated Dr. Young.

JOHN RYAN, *cons.* 1825; *ob.* 1864.

John Ryan, late Bishop of Limerick, son of Patrick Ryan and Catherine Hickey, was born on the 9th of November, 1784,* in the little village of Burris, in the parish of Two-mile Burris, near Thurles, county Tipperary.† He received his early education at a good school in Thurles, and entered Maynooth for logic, Sept. 10, 1807. His college course was an unusually short one, owing to the wants of the diocese. Passing

---

* The date of birth is taken from the registry at Maynooth, filled up probably from Dr. Ryan's baptismal certificate. The parish books of Burris were destroyed by fire about 40 years ago.

† The present much-respected parish priest of Two-mile Burris and Moykarkey, the Very Rev. John Burke, is Dr. Ryan's nephew.

over physics, and reading theology for only two years, he was ordained sub-deacon, deacon, and priest at the Pentecost retreat, 1810, in the college chapel, by the Most Rev. Dr. Murray, then coadjutor of Dublin. After leaving Maynooth he was appointed to the curacy of Doon in his native diocese. But he served there for only a few months, when an opportunity offered of improving his mind by further study and travel. At the request of Archbishop Bray, he accompanied on the Continent as governor a young gentleman of the first Catholic family in the city of Limerick. The time spent on this tour, a little less than two years, he employed in adding to his own acquirements, and forming the mind and habits of his pupil.

"With Dr. Ryan, bishop of Limerick", writes the late James Roche, the octogenarian essayist, "I have been for many years most intimately acquainted, for he was travelling tutor to one of my nephews, who owes everything to his care and kindness. I am myself, though reputed a Cork man, a native of Limerick, of which my brother William was the first Catholic representative; he was succeeded by my nephew, John O'Brien. I left home in early boyhood for a foreign education, to which every Catholic of any position in society was then compelled to resort. Unhappily the same necessity exists still. I suffered much in order to learn the little I know. I witnessed the French revolution of 1789, where I was imprisoned for a long time, and again in 1831 I was present at the inauguration of Louis Philippe. Thus my life has been passed abroad, but I have had many opportunities of becoming acquainted with nearly all the bishops of the south of Ireland for the greater part of a century, many of whom I remember as most welcome guests at my father's house".

On his return, Dr. Ryan resumed his humble curacy at Doon, and laboured in it zealously until the death of F. M'Knight, the parish priest, when he was appointed to succeed in his stead. Not long after he was translated to the then united parishes of Mullinahone and Drangan.

Towards the end of 1824, Dr. Tuohy finding the duties of his sacred office above his strength, urgently pressed the Holy See to grant him a coadjutor, naming for this office the Rev. F. Joseph O'Finan, O.P., the Very Rev. John M'Enery, P.P., Tralee and V.G. of Kerry, and the Rev. John Ryan, P.P. of Mullinahone. Fr. O'Finan opposed from the beginning his own election, perhaps for the reasons given already, but more probably on higher personal grounds. Dr. Tuohy referred the Cardinal of Propaganda for the character of the other two distinguished priests to their respective bishops. On May 28, 1825, the Pro-Prefect, Cardinal Somalia, wrote to Dr. Egan of Kerry, requesting his opinion of the fitness of "John Maurice M'Enery, a priest of his diocese, recommended by the bishop of Limerick for his coadjutor". A like letter had been despatched some time before to Archbishop Laffan, and Dr. Tuohy informed his Grace on May 26, same year, that he had earnestly solicited the appointment of Mr. Ryan, and asked the Cardinal of Propaganda to consult his Grace on the subject. The letter concludes with a request that the Archbishop will report favourably of Dr. Ryan's merits, further delay being now most inconvenient. We have no copy of Dr. Egan's answer, but we may well conjecture what it must have been. The late parish priest of Tralee won universal respect by his learning and piety, and he was a special favourite with his bishop. Dr. Laffan warmly recommended Mr. Ryan, and this well-deserved testimony probably decided the Court of Rome in his favour. Dr. Ryan was nominated coadjutor of Limerick, with right of succession by the Congregation of Propaganda on the 25th September, 1825, and approved by the Pope on the same day. October 15th, 1825, Cardinal Somaglia enclosed to the Archbishop of Cashel a letter for Dr. Ryan, announcing his appointment as *Episcopus Myriensis in partibus.* His Bulls reached Limerick before the end of October, and he was consecrated in St. John's Chapel, Limerick, on Sunday, 11th of December, 1825, by Dr. Laffan, Archbishop of Cashel, assisted by Dr. Tuohy, and Dr. Kelly of Waterford. The Very Rev. Dean M'Namara preached the sermon. On the evening of the consecration, the priests of the diocese, at their own special request, had the honour of entertaining the new prelate and his friends, thus effectually stopping a mischievous rumour, that they were opposed to the introduction of a stranger over them. Resistance to bishops appointed by the Holy See is a crime of which Irish Church history furnishes few examples.

In order to show the great advance of religion while Dr. Ryan ruled the diocese, it would be only necessary to name the pious foundations in Limerick city and county, from his consecration in 1825, to his death in 1864. In this list would be comprised every charitable institute in the diocese, except the Christian Brothers' Schools, established as we have seen under his venerable predecessor. In 1825 there was but one convent of nuns, the Poor Clares, in the whole diocese, and even that one failed afterwards. How many convents have been founded since then? The Presentation Convent, in 1837; Mercy Convents— Limerick city, A.D. 1848; Newcastle West, the next year; Rathkeale, 1850; Adair, 1854; Convent of the Faithful Companions, in Laurel Hill, 1846; a branch of the same order at Bruff, 1856; Convent of the Good Shepherd, first established by nuns from Angers, in 1849. The Redemptorist Fathers introduced into Limerick, November 30th, 1853, began their convent—the only one of the order still in Ireland—in 1856, and the beautiful new Church of St. Alphonsus, in 1858. The learned Fathers of the Society opened their schools in Limerick, on March 10th, 1859. All these institutions were not merely planted by the Right Rev. Dr. Ryan; they were supported by him, and brought forth abundant fruit under his fostering care.*

There is not, perhaps, a city of its wealth and extent in the empire better provided than Limerick is now with pious communities, and these communities are all well endowed and thriving, and likely to become more useful. The contrast between the city of by-gone days and the city of to-day is admirably brought out by the Venerable Dean O'Brien in his eloquent sermon at the Month's Mind of the late Bishop:

" Four-and-forty years ago there were not in Limerick city—with a population as great as at present—there were not at school *three hundred* children of both sexes. There are a good many over *four thousand* to-day. To whom is the change mainly due? To the Right Rev. Dr. Ryan . . . Four-and-forty years ago we had not one single institution of benevolence—no orphanage—no house of refuge—no home for the unfortunate—no monastery, convent, or good school. Look at them to-day. Over seventy nuns instruct and watch over our poor girls; thirty monks bestow their time, talents, and zeal

* More details will be found in the full and extremely accurate *History of Limerick*, by Mr. Lenihan.

upon over two thousand young boys; four-and-twenty companions of Jesus preside over the improvement of the middle classes, and impart to the higher classes a perfect education. The Jesuits, those great masters of intellectual and moral culture, watch over the most exalted sphere of mental progress; and four or five-and-twenty ladies devote their lives to the recovery of fallen and degraded women from sin and crime".

Among the great material works associated with the bishop's name, and most deserving of record, is the magnificent cathedral of St. John, the first stone of which was laid by the Right Rev. Dr. Ryan, on the 1st of May, 1856.*

His edition of the diocesan statutes was published in 1842. In the preface he gives a short account of the labours of his pious predecessors :

" Not unmindful of his duty (to promote discipline), the Most Illustrious and Most Rev. Cornelius O'Keeffe, who was elected bishop of Limerick in 1720, after the storm of persecution that raged in this country for many years had somewhat subsided, made it his first care to restore ecclesiastical discipline, and draw up new rules, which he published the next year, and approved by his authority.

" These constitutions, sanctioned by long usage, his successor, the Most Rev. Robert Lacy, ratified with additional statutes regarding the publication of banns and the offering for Masses. On his decease the Most Rev. Daniel O'Kearney was elected to succeed him. Having been more than once assailed by the importunity and threats of influential laymen, who sought the promotion to parishes of unfit and unworthy priests, he determined to free himself and his successors from such annoyance, and made a statute, by virtue of which priests seeking to obtain benefices through lay intervention, were made incapable of all promotion in the diocese. He also received the decree of Trent, annulling clandestine marriages, which he ordered to be published throughout the diocese in 1775.

* An accurate description of this magnificent temple is given by Mr. Lenihan.

"Finally the Right Rev. Denis Conway, his successor, lessened the number of reserved cases, and increased the offering for Masses. These statutes, of which some old copies are still extant, but transcribed most inaccurately, we thought proper to put in order and to print more correctly; others, required by the circumstances of the present time, we have added in our Provincial synods".

In this collection there are, together with very many excellent counsels, some practical decisions which need to be modified considerably. The decree in p. 43, that the sick can receive the Holy Viaticum *only once a week*, is one which a bishop should not attempt to define, according to Benedict XIV., *de Synodo*, lib. vii. c. xii., n. 5: abstrahat igitur episcopus ab hisce questionibus; solumque parochis insinuet posse et debere sanctissimum Viaticum in eadem infirmitate iterum et tertio administrari. To the sick, *not fasting* (for of them alone can any doubt arise), if otherwise *well disposed*, we would have no scruple in allowing daily Communion; and this is, we have reason to know, the practice at Rome.* Is the pious believer who fed on Christ's body as his *daily* bread for years, to be deprived of this comfort in his last struggle? The rule for the form (*ibid.*), semel tantum in eadem morbo *per modum viatici*, is against the authority of the best rubricists, who teach that the form "*Accipe*, etc.", is to be always used while the mortal sickness continues. Even when the sick are *fasting*, but still *in danger of death*, accipe, etc., is the proper form.† The decree that the sick shall be anointed but *once in the same sickness*, seems to ex-

* See Dean O'Kane's learned and accurate work on the Rubrics, No. 775. "But it is a very probable opinion, maintained by many, that Communion may be delivered [to the sick not fasting] the next day, and even every day".

† *Ibid.*, No. 779, "We think it more probable, that while the danger continues, the form should be always *Accipe*, etc.".

tend to cases of *long-continued sickness*, and so is against the practice of the most zealous priests even in Rome, who do not hesitate to anoint again after a month in the same sickness. What abuse could justify a threat of suspension against a priest for no other crime but giving a gospel (as it is termed) to any person not of his own flock ? These little blots we should not notice, but they touch on points eminently practical: sunt delicta tamen quibus ignovisse velimus.

To the statutes is added an appendix containing the resolutions of the Munster Bishops at Fermoy, 6th of May, 1828, and the decrees of several popes against freemasons.

All the panegyrists of the late bishop have been obliged to make an apology for some of his views. They admit that he differed widely not only from the people under his care, but even from the majority of the Irish prelates, on some important questions, political and religious. As one instance, we may refer to the education measure proposed by Sir Robert Peel's Government in 1845. Dr. Ryan signed the resolutions and memorial adopted at the general meeting of the bishops in Dublin, May 23rd, 1845, and again joined in the sentence passed at Maynooth, 25th June, 1845, declaring the new education scheme *dangerous to faith and morals*. But when the Government made some slight concessions, he was less opposed to the bill in its amended form; and it is well known that he voted against the final condemnation of the Queen's Colleges at the national synod of Thurles, although the securities demanded by the Irish bishops in their memorial had been refused. That he and the few prelates who dissented from their brethren were deceived by false hopes, is quite certain. But can we suspect their motives? What did Dr. Ryan ever gain by siding with the Government? Of all the Irish bishops there was not one who spoke out his mind more fearlessly, whatever party was in power, Whig or Tory. Before a general council, he would have declared his sentiments as freely, yet deliberately and calmly, as before the humblest curate in his diocese. And what was better, the freedom he claimed for himself, and used on all occasions with unshrinking manliness, he allowed without stint or measure to those who differed from him. He was wrong on the University question, but he was sincere, and his motives pure. Above all things, writes Cardinal Fransoni, in his famous rescript condemning the "godless" colleges, " we feel bound to say that this Congregation never suspected those prelates who seemed to favour the establishment of the colleges; for their probity is known to us by long experience, and we are well aware that they were influenced only by the hope of greater good, and of advancing the interests of religion".

. Although Dr. Ryan was scrupulously exact in discharging his duties within his own diocese, he never failed to take part in the councils—provincial and national—of his brother prelates. Examples of his zeal in this respect from the subject before us are abundant. He attended at the month's mind of Dr. Collins, Bishop of Cloyne, at Fermoy, 15th January, 1833; left on most pressing business before the nomination on 16th, Drs. Murphy (Cork), and Egan (Kerry), remaining. The three names chosen were: Very Rev. Dr. O'Connell, Vicar-Capitular, Very Rev.

Drs. Crotty and Walsh. He signed the joint recommendation of the bishops of the province in favour of Dr. Crotty, who was elected bishop.

1834, December 15th.—Attended at Newmarket-on Fergus, where were also Drs. Slattery, Murphy, Egan, and M'Mahon, with forty-five parish priests, all in the diocese but three (sick). The priests nominated Patrick Kennedy, parish priest, Birr; Charles Fahy, parish priest, Tulla; Daniel Vaughan, parish priest, Killaloe. Dr. Kennedy, supported by the bishops, was appointed to Killaloe.

1837, February 22nd.—Thirty-two parish priests assembled at Waterford, together with Drs. Ryan, Egan, and Kennedy; Dominick O'Brien, Secretary, Peter Walsh and James Hally, Scrutators. They postulated for N. Foran, parish priest, Dungarvan; G. Connolly, Carrick-on-Suir; and Michael Tobin, Cahir. Bishops warmly recommended Dr. Foran, as they did before on November 12th, 1829, when the see was vacant.

I do not know, indeed, one provincial or national synod from which Dr. Ryan was absent down to 1860, when his health failed. It was specially noted that he and his venerable friend, the Bishop of Raphoe, were both absent from the general meeting of bishops, April, 1861. He was also a trustee of Maynooth College since 1847, and assisted most punctually at the college board.

The first public notice of Dr. Ryan's intention to ask for a coadjutor appeared in a Dublin paper, April 10th, 1860. The nomination took place on the 2nd of May, when the three priests recommended were: Dean Butler, Dr. Cussen, Dr. O'Reilly, S J.

Dr. Butler's appointment was publicly announced

in the press at the end of May, 1861, and he was consecrated on the 25th of July following. He had been a great favourite of the old bishop, who gave him all his own authority even as to the collation of benefices, etc., and the same good fortune continued to attend him for a long time after his election as coadjutor. But towards the end of Dr. Ryan's life, when it was generally believed his mind was weakened by age and sickness, a painful incident occurred, which caused no little trouble in the diocese. After the death of the Ven. Archdeacon Fitzgerald, Feb. 6, 1863, Dr. Ryan collated his own relative, the Rev. James Hickey, parish priest Donoughmore, to the vacant parish. To this appointment Dr. Butler objected, chiefly, we believe, on the ground that Fr. Hickey had no fair claim to be thus raised above other priests of much longer standing and higher merit, and he promoted the Rev. James Raleigh, parish priest of Askeaton, the most deserving priest, perhaps, in the diocese, to Rathkeale. After appeal to Rome Fr. Hickey was ordered to give in his formal resignation to the Archbishop of Cashel. Fr. Raleigh then took quiet possession of the parish, and the whole question seemed to be settled peaceably; not so, however. On the following Saturday evening he went on important business to Askeaton, intending to return in time for Mass next morning. On his way back to the chapel on Sunday he learned that the chapel gates were closed, and that a strong body of men within the church were resolved to refuse him admission. There was no Mass that Sunday, nor on several Sundays after. The leaders of the discontented party waited on Dr. Butler to represent the wishes of the people. His Lordship received them courteously, and explained how impossible it was for him to alter arrangements that had been made at Rome To that supreme authority bishops, priests, and people should humbly submit. Not awed by this calm and reasonable appeal, the deputies organized a strong force to march to Park House, where the old bishop was then lying in his bed of sickness At the gate of the bishop's house Fr. Hickey met them, and implored of them to leave the issue in the hands of those whom God had appointed to rule the Church. Neither he, nor Dr. Butler, nor Dr. Ryan, could set aside the final decision of the Sacred Congregation. All this remonstrance was also vain. The church at Rathkeale was still closed. Fr. Raleigh and his curates did not interfere, in the hope that the good people, hitherto devotedly attached to their priests, would soon see their error and be brought back to a sense of duty. This forbearance had the desired effect, for on the 8th of September the keys of the church were quietly delivered up to Fr. Raleigh, and among the first to confess their guilt and to seek forgiveness were the ringleaders of this unmeaning revolt. After this unpleasant contest the whole administration of the diocese was left to Dr. Butler, who appointed Fr. Hickey to the parish of Askeaton, the just reward of his unqualified and edifying submission. We must add the instructive lesson, that not only the aged bishop, but also the two parish priests, Frs. Raleigh and Hickey, have already passed to their everlasting rest.

Dr. Ryan departed this life a little before one o'clock A.M. on Monday, June 6, 1864. On the day before about noon the last fatal symptoms appeared.

" All that respect and affection could dictate was, it need

not be said, contributed to smooth his downward physical path to the tomb. Little was needed. Tranquilly the good bishop went to his mortal sleep, and without a struggle which would move a feature, he breathed his last".—*Munster News.*

His remains were removed in public procession on Tuesday evening to the cathedral, and buried on Wednesday before the High Altar, after the usual solemn offices for the dead, The Most Rev. Dr. Leahy, archbishop of Cashel, singing the High Mass, and the Right Rev. Dr. Butler giving the last absolution. On the coffin plate was this simple inscription: "Right Rev. John Ryan, Lord Bishop of Limerick, died on the 6th of June, 1864, in the 81st year of his age, and the 39th of his episcopacy".* Dr. Ryan left his means, which were, we believe, considerable, for charitable purposes, appointing as his executors the Most Rev. Dr. Butler, and the Right Hon. William Monsell, M.P. (now Lord Emly).

GEORGE BUTLER, *cons.* 1861; *diu sospes sit.*

George Butler, son of George Butler and Mary Kilbride, was born in Thomond Gate, city of Limerick, February 13, 1815.† In 1829 he went to the diocesan academy, then under the direction of the Rev. Dr. Carey, a pious and learned secular priest of the diocese of Killaloe, on whose death he entered Maynooth College for rhetoric, February 4, 1832.

After winning the highest literary honours during his course, he was promoted to the Dunboyne establishment, June 25, 1838. His brother, John, who

---

* Dr. Ryan died in his 80th year, according to the entry in the Maynooth registry, which was made, we have no doubt, from the baptismal certificate taken from the parish books.
† Baptized by the Rev. Richard Walsh, P.P., Thomond Gate.

matriculated for the rhetoric class, Maynooth, August 25, 1831, was also a Dunboyne student of the previous year.

In the autumn of 1838, the Right Rev. R. P. Smith, Coadjutor Bishop of Trinidad, in the West Indies, went to Maynooth, hoping to find there some zealous young students with the heart to follow him to his distant and dangerous mission. The first to offer their services were the brothers, John and George Butler, who were soon joined by the Rev. Thomas Butler, Dublin, the Rev. John Gallagher, Kilmore, the Rev. Christopher Fagan, Meath, and two younger students.

Dr. Smith's great scheme was to found a college in Trinidad, to place it under the care of well-qualified priests, and so provide for the religious and educational wants of his diocese. We may well imagine the joy of the good bishop on securing the services of these generous young men, so well fitted for the work on which he had set his heart. With redoubled zeal he now urged on his preparations. However desponding he may have been hitherto, he could hardly fail to conceive strong hopes from this successful beginning.

On the 26th of November, 1838, John and George Butler were ordained priests in the junior chapel, Maynooth College, by the Right Rev. Dr. Smith, and early in November they sailed for the West Indies. During the voyage, which was unusually long and difficult, they met with hardships not always caused by adverse winds. On arriving at Trinidad, they were kindly received by the aged bishop, the Right Rev. Dr. M'Donnell, who told them at once frankly that, though ready to give the new college all the support he could, and well aware of its necessity, he could hardly hope for success in a place where primary education was still so backward. The college project was in truth conceived by Dr. Smith. Dr. M'Donnell heard very little of it, except in some casual conversation, yet he was too honourable a man to withdraw from the promises of his coadjutor, or break faith with those young priests who came out to Trinidad for the purpose of being employed chiefly in the work of education. Though little progress could be made in the absence of Dr. Smith, who was still detained in London on important business, yet Dr. M'Donnell opened the school at once, and placed it under the care of the Rev. John Butler, who also acted as chaplain to St. Joseph's Convent. For a time the college, as it was called, prospered apace. The number of pupils was never very large, but the average attendance was higher than could have been well expected. The Rev. John Butler, ably assisted by his brother, devoted his whole energies to the interests of the school, but he did not live to reap the full reward of his zeal. In about nine months he died of fever, brought on by anxiety and overwork.

By a rare fate Dr. George Butler was not permitted to close his brother's eyes in death. On the very day before, he was summoned to a distant part of the island to administer the last rites of the Church to a poor sufferer who could not see any other priest.

At this time a fearful pestilence broke out, which spread rapidly through the island; the college was closed in consequence, and the priests hitherto emgaged in teaching were all employed in missionary duty. One of the first victims of the prevailing malady was a zealous and distinguished Irish priest, the Rev. Mr. Duffy, in whose place Dr. George Butler was appointed curé of San Fernando. Being now released from the only earthly tie that bound him to that strange land, Dr. Butler resolved only the more earnestly to spend himself in the service of the souls committed to his care.

" Within less than a year he had three severe attacks of fever. Having heard of these circumstances, the Right Rev. Dr. Ryan signified his wish that the Rev. George Butler should return to Limerick. In obedience to that wish— for Dr. Ryan was still his bishop—the young missionary left the West Indies, and arrived in Limerick towards the end of 1840, when he was appointed to the curacy of St. Patrick's. In St. Patrick's the Rev. George Butler continued curate for four years, at the end of which he was sent to St. Michael's, where he was curate for twelve years, during the last years of which he was administrator. In 1857 he was appointed parish priest of St. Mary's and dean of the diocese".†

The first public notice of any meeting to nominate a coadjutor in Limerick appeared in a Dublin paper, April 10, 1860, which gave a circumstantial account of a chapter of the clergy on Holy Thursday, April 5, and the names of the three candidates recommended. But this story turned out to be a lucky guess, or rather a foregone conclusion. The priests spoke probably on the matter when they came together on Holy Thursday; the election did not take place until the 2nd of May, when the clergy met in St. John's Cathedral, and nominated in the first place the Very Rev. Dean Butler; in the second, Dr. Cussen, P.P., Bruff; and in the third, the Very Rev. E. O'Reilly, S.J. We need hardly say that the

† Mr. Lenihan's *History of Limerick*, p. 642. Dr. Butler left the Port of Spain on the 1st of August, 1840, and reached Limerick about the middle of September following.

clergy of Limerick honoured themselves by their choice of these three priests.

Towards the end of May a local paper contained this paragraph: "It is confidently asserted, and we believe with truth, that the Very Rev. Dean Butler is appointed by the Supreme Authority coadjutor bishop of the diocese of Limerick". This announcement was, however, premature. The appointment was then certain, but had not taken place.

The Bull naming Dr. Butler coadjutor of Limerick, with right of succession, is dated June 18th, 1861. He was consecrated in St. John's Cathedral, Limerick, on the 25th July, 1861, by the Most Rev. Dr. Leahy, Archbishop of Cashel, assisted by the Right Rev. Dr. Keane of Cloyne and the Right Rev. Dr. Flannery of Killaloe. His Lordship the Bishop of Kerry preached the consecration sermon. Among the other prelates present were: His Grace the Archbishop of Dublin; the Most Rev. Bishops of Clogher (M'Nally), Elphin, Galway, Ross, Kilfenora, Hyderabad (Murphy), Bombay (Whelan), and the Archimandrite of Lebanon.

The venerable bishop of the diocese, Dr. Ryan, did not take part in the ceremony through delicate health, though he sat for a short time at dinner, at which were fourteen bishops and one hundred and eighty priests.

On the 6th of June, 1864, Dr. Butler succeeded to the see of Limerick. His Lordship is still in the prime of life, with the prospect of many useful, and we trust happy, years before him.

www.ingramcontent.com/pod-product-compliance
Lightning Source LLC
Chambersburg PA
CBHW032158160426
43197CB00008B/971